Ian McEwan

麦克尤恩 双语作品

蟑 螂
The Cockroach

〔英〕伊恩·麦克尤恩——著
宋佥——译

上海译文出版社

蟑螂

前　言

感谢一位接一位的英国首相锲而不舍、毫不松口的谈判，感谢议会的混乱与瘫痪、两场大选以及整个国家的痛苦分裂，大不列颠近年来正努力要实现英伦列岛有史以来最无聊、最受虐狂的一项追求。英国之外的整个世界——普京与川普两位总统除外——全都惊愕地在一旁看着。如果我们真的成功脱欧了，接下来我们就将开启未来十五年的艰苦跋涉，希望能回头重拾一鳞半爪我们曾经拥有的那一切——许许多多的贸易协定，安全与科研合作，还有其他成千上万种便利的协议。我们为什么要对自己做这样的事情？我的蟑螂首相给了德国总理那个唯一可能的答案：因为。

在这个历史进程中，《蟑螂》的构思正是发生在那个绝望与大笑交会的关头。许多人会觉得，也许脱欧的进程是无法付诸讽喻的。什么样的邪恶小说家能想出来这样的事情呢？这件事本身就是一出曲折的自我讽喻。也许，留给我们的只剩下嘲弄和大笑的悲哀慰藉了吧。

无论我们的脱欧时刻最终是否会到来，有一些问题将是未来很长一段时间里我们都要问自己的。谎言、可疑的献金、俄国的介入都将是未来的历史学家们的关注点所在。他们也一定会研究一种特殊的"魔粉"所导致的失明——在当下席卷欧洲、美国、巴西、印度和许多其他国家的所有那些民粹运动中，这种"魔粉"可谓是一种共性。"魔粉"的成分在如今已是人尽皆知：疯狂的非理性、对陌生人的敌意、抵制耐心的分析、怀疑"专家"、夜郎自大式的爱国、狂热地相信简单粗暴的解决办法、渴求文化上的"纯洁"——再加入一小撮利用这些冲动的无底线政客。

当然，各地的情况有所不同。在巴西，他们喜欢焚烧亚马孙雨林。美国渴望建成它的墨西哥墙。土耳其将监禁记者的技艺打磨得炉火纯青。在英国，在这"魔粉"让我们闭上眼睛的时刻，我们也发现了欧盟的生态进化如何深刻地塑造了我们本国的植被风貌。将这些植被连根拔起愈发证明是一个暴戾的过程,而且——归根结底——并不十分简单。可这没有吓住任何人。我们会奋勇向前——因为。

英国确实存在着许多历史上的不公,可那些不公极少来自欧盟。脱欧派的任务就是让选民相信完全相反的结论。他们以百分之三十七的支持率成功了,这件事足以改变我们在未来许多年里的集体命运。凭借着经典的民粹主义"魔粉",脱欧派对冲基金老板、财阀、伊顿公学学生与报业大亨将自己打造成精英阶层的敌人。这办法奏效了,现在这群反精英的精英组成了我们的政府。

在英国政治讽喻的文学传统中,奠基性的文本依然是乔纳森·斯威夫特的《一个温和的建议》。我第一次读这篇文章的时候只有十六岁。作者在文中面不改色地断言活吃婴儿能够解决一个长期存在的难题,这话听上去真是既野蛮又怪诞,可并不比——在斯威夫特看来——英国在爱尔兰的统治更残酷。

而在英国脱欧这出戏中，某种丑恶怪异的东西进入了我们的政治精神中，因此，对我而言，召唤出蟑螂——所有生命形式中最受鄙视的一种——就似乎是顺理成章了。对于任何想象人虫换体的文学尝试而言，卡夫卡的《变形记》都是怎么也绕不过的；不过，在鞠躬表达必要的致敬之后，斯威夫特才是我转而求助的对象。我的任务始终是构思出一个政治与经济计划，其适得其反的荒诞性能够与脱欧相提并论。我不知道我那个荒唐的杜撰——"反转主义"——算不算得上成功。有鉴于眼下这个国家计划的规模及其对至少未来一代人可能造成的冲击，也许没有什么能够在愚蠢的尺度上和它匹敌。

接近三分之二的英国选民没有投票支持脱欧。大部分商业、农业、科学、金融与人文从业者反对脱欧计划。四分之三的议员投票支持留在欧盟，但他们大多忽视了公共利益，躲在了党派站队和"人民发话了"后面——那句冷冰冰的苏联式口号，那团笼罩头脑的"魔尘"，它蒙蔽了理性，黯淡了我们的子孙后代未来在大陆欧洲自由工作生活的前景。

民粹主义——它对自身的无知浑然不觉，满嘴嘟囔着血与土，满心不切实际的本土保护主义渴求和对气候变化的可悲轻蔑——在未来也许还会召唤出别的怪物，其中一些要远比英国脱欧更暴力，后果也更严重。但在民粹的所有版本中，蟑螂的精神都将发扬光大。我们应该好好了解这种生物，这样才能更好地击败它。我相信我们会的。

如果理性不能睁开双眼，最终胜出，那么我们也许就只能仰赖笑声了。

献给蒂莫西·加顿·艾什[①]

① 蒂莫西·加顿·艾什（1955— ），英国牛津大学欧洲研究教授，以对中东欧现当代史的研究蜚声学界，是西方极具影响力的知识分子。

本中篇小说纯属虚构。人名与人物出自作者想象,任何与现实蟑螂(无论在世与否)的相似点都纯属巧合。

那天早上，吉姆·萨姆斯——一个脑瓜聪明但全无深度的家伙——从不安的梦境中醒来，赫然发现自己变成了一头庞然大物。有好一会儿，他仰面朝天（这可不是他最爱的姿势）躺在那里，遥望着他的脚掌和少得可怜的几条腿，心中愕然。区区四条，毫无疑问，而且很不灵活。换作是他自己的那几条棕色的小长腿——他已经开始有些怀念它们了——这时一定早就开始在半空中欢快地舞蹈了，无论那舞姿有多么绝望。他一动不动地躺着，告诉自己不要恐慌。一个器官——一块滑溜溜的肉——卡在他的嘴里，扁扁的，湿湿的，恶心得要命，尤其是这东西自己会动，四出探索着他那山洞一般的巨大口腔，而当它滑过一大排大牙时，他嘴上不出声，心中又是一惊。他凝视着自己的整副躯干。从肩膀到脚踝，他的体色呈淡蓝色，脖子和腕部周围有圈深蓝色的滚边，一排白色的纽扣沿着他没有分节的胸部一字纵向排列。一阵时起时停的轻风拂过那里，带来了一股腐烂食物和谷酿酒精的诱人味道，他猜测这就是他的呼吸了。他的视野狭隘得无可救药——哎，没法儿和复眼比——看到的一切都色彩斑斓得让他压抑。他开始渐渐意识到，出于某种古怪的反转，他脆弱的肉体现在翻到了骨骼的外头，将那骨骼彻彻底底隐藏了起来。他多么渴望能再看一眼他那亲切的、泛着光泽的棕色外壳啊。

这一切已经够叫他发愁的了，可随着他的脑子渐渐苏醒，他还想起了自己正在独自执行一项重大任务，尽管他一时记不得那任务是什么了。我要迟到了，他想着，一面努力从枕头上抬起一颗能有五公斤重的脑袋。这不公平，他自语道。凭什么让我来受这份罪。方才他那破碎的梦境深沉而狂野，充斥回响着喧嚣刺耳、争执不休的各种声音。直到现在，当这颗脑袋重重地落回枕头上的时候，他的视线才开始穿透迷雾，望向梦境的尽头，脑中回想起了一堆彼此交织的记忆、印象与动机,而当他试图抓住它们的时候,这堆马赛克却立刻分崩离析。

是的,他离开了那散发着怡人的腐败气息的议会大厦,甚至没有告别。他只能如此。保密要紧。他对此了然于心,无需言明。可他究竟是何时出发的?一定是在天黑之后。是昨天夜里?还是前天夜里?他一定是走地下车库出去的。他应该绕过了门口那个警察锃亮的皮靴。现在他想起来了。顺着阴沟,他一路小跑,一直跑到议会广场上那个可怕的十字路口边。在一列空转着引擎、急不可耐地要把他在沥青路面上碾作齑粉的汽车前面,他以百米冲刺的速度奔进了马路对面的阴沟。在那之后,他似乎又花了一个星期的时间才穿过又一条可怕的马路,来到白厅街上他该去的那一面。再然后呢?他一定又飞奔了许多码,然后停下了脚步。为什么?现在他渐渐想起来了。身上的每一根气管都喘着粗气,他停在了一条沁人心脾的下水道边,在一片被人丢弃的披萨上用起了点心。他当然吃不完,可他尽力了。他运气很好,那是一片玛格丽塔,他的次爱。没有橄榄。那一片上没有。

他现在发现,他这颗笨重的脑袋却可以毫不费力地一百八十度旋转。他把它转向了一侧。这是一间小小的顶楼卧室,被早晨的阳光照得通亮,煞是讨厌,因为窗帘没有拉。他的床头有一部电话——不,两部电话。他视野有限的目光扫过地毯,落在了踢脚板下沿的一道窄缝上。我一定是在晨光中从那下面挤进来的,他悻悻地想。我本可以过着幸福的生活。屋子的另一头是一张沙发,边上有一张矮桌,上面摆着一只雕花平底玻璃杯和一个空了的威士忌酒瓶。一把扶手椅上铺陈着一件西服和一件熨平叠好的衬衣。窗边的一张大桌子上放着两盒文件,一盒叠在另一盒上面,全是红盒子。

现在他转起眼珠子来愈发地驾轻就熟了,因为他理解了两只眼球无需人为干预就能平顺地同步转动。他还发现,与其让舌头耷拉在两片嘴唇外头,时不时地往胸口上滴两滴口水,还不如把它收进湿漉漉的口腔里头来得舒服些。真可怕。可他开始逐渐掌握驾驭这个新形体的诀窍了。他一向学得很快。他真正操心的还是他必须着手履行他的使命这件事。他有几个重要的决定要做。忽然,地板上的一道影子吸引了他的注意力。那是一个小动物,有着他自己原先的形体,那无疑正是此刻被他鸠占鹊巢的这副躯壳的旧主人。他饶有兴致、不无爱怜地看着那个小东西奋力翻过绒毛地毯的线头,朝门口爬去。到了那里它犹豫着,两根触须举棋不定地摇摆着,举手投足处处流露出一个新手的笨拙。终于,它鼓足勇气,颤巍巍地从门板下面的缝隙里钻了出去,开启了一段艰辛坎坷、危机四伏的下山路。回议会大厦的长路漫漫,路上险象环生。但如果它能走到终点,没有被人在脚底下踩成肉饼,它将在大厦的镶板墙后面和木地板下面,在它千千万万个兄弟姐妹中间找到安全和慰藉。他祝它好运。可现在,他必须料理他自己的事情了。

但吉姆依然一动不动。这一切都全无道理,一切行动都毫无意义,除非他能拼凑出将他引入一间陌生卧房的那趟旅程，那些事件。吃完那顿天降的大餐后他一路疾行，几乎没有注意到头顶的喧嚣，全神贯注于他自己的事情，寸步不离阴沟的荫蔽，尽管他已经想不起来自己行了多远，跑了多久了。他能够肯定的就是，最终他来到了一个高耸入天的障碍物前——一座小粪山，尚有余温，隐隐冒着热气。换作是平时，他一定会欢呼雀跃的。他自认为也算得上是个鉴赏家。他懂得如何生活精致。这样特别的好货他一闻便知。那股坚果味的芳香，兼有些许汽油、香蕉皮和洗革皂的味道，绝对错不了。皇家骑兵卫队！可他已经在两餐之间进过食了，真是大错特错啊。那片玛格丽塔让他对排泄物完全没了胃口，无论那是多么新鲜和上乘的排泄物；同时鉴于他愈来愈疲惫的身体，他也根本不想翻山越岭。他蹲伏在粪山的背阴中，脚踏山麓松弹的土地，考虑着他的选择。沉思了片刻后，他清楚了自己该怎么做。他开始攀爬路边石那竖直的花岗岩壁，打算绕过粪堆，绕到山的另一头再爬下来。

此刻，斜倚在这间阁楼卧室里，他认定就在那一刻，他告别了他的自由意志——或是自由意志的幻觉，被一种更伟大的、高瞻远瞩的力量所左右。当他登上人行道时，他向那集体的精魂臣服了。他只是一个宏大计划中微不足道的一分子，这个计划的尺度超出了任何个体的理解范畴。

他奋力攀上路边石的上沿，发现那坨粪便在人行道上绵延了三分之一个路面。就在这时，突如其来的一场风暴晴空霹雳般地落在了他头上——成千上万双脚踩踏的隆隆声，口号声与铃铛声，口哨声与喇叭声。又一场吵闹的游行示威。在这样的深夜。粗野之徒在本该老实待在家里的时候出来惹麻烦。如今，这些抗议活动几乎每星期都有。干扰重要的公共服务，妨碍体面的老百姓从事合法的活动。他站在路边石上，呆若木鸡，以为自己随时会被一脚踩扁。尺码足有他自身体长十五倍的大鞋底砰然落地，离他蜷缩之处只有几英寸远，震得他的触须和人行道路面一起瑟瑟发抖。万幸的是，就在那时，他选择了抬头仰望，纯粹是出于一种宿命论的情愫。他准备好了迎接死亡。可也正是在那一刻，他看到了机会——游行队列中现出了一个缺口。下一拨抗议者还在五十码开外。他看到了他们的横幅在飘扬,他们的旗帜在逼近——一片蓝底上的许多黄色的星星。还有米字旗。他这辈子从没有跑这么快过。体节中的每一根气管都喘着粗气,他终于跑到了对面一扇沉重的铁门前,只差几秒钟人群那可怕的脚步就要再度从他头上轰隆隆地践踏而过了,现在还多了此起彼伏的嘘声和野蛮的鼓点声。心中满是极度的恐惧和愤慨——一对不协调的组合——他冲下人行道,钻过铁门,只求保命,钻进了一条小路的庇护与宁静之中。他立刻在这里认出了一只标配警靴的后跟。令人宽心,一如既往。

然后呢?他沿着空荡荡的人行道走着,走过一排高级住宅。他来这里一定是符合计划的。他的族类的集体潜意识信息素①赋予了他一种对于前进方向的本能认知。平安无事地又走了半个小时的路后,他停下了脚步,本该如此。街对面

---

① 信息素,生物体释放的一种化学物质,能为一定距离外的同种生物察觉并影响其行为。

聚集着上百名摄影师和记者。街这边，他来到了一扇门前，与门齐平，门外又站着一个警察。就在这时，门忽然开了，一个穿高跟鞋的女人跨出门来，差点在他腹部第九节和第十节上钻了个洞。门依然开着。也许有访客要来。就在那短短几秒钟里，吉姆透过大门，看见了一个亲切好客、灯光柔和的门厅，墙面的踢脚板有点破损——这永远是个好兆头。一股冲动突然攫住了他——他现在知道了那冲动并非源自他自己——他跑了进去。

有鉴于他不同寻常的处境，躺在一张陌生的床上，他的发挥已经很不错了，还能回忆起这样的细节。他的大脑，他的意识差不多仍然是先前的老样子，这可真是件让人高兴的事儿。毕竟，他留住了他的本我。进屋后他没有朝踢脚板的方向跑去，而是逃向了楼梯，而造成这一切的都是一只赫然出现、令他始料未及的猫。他爬上三级台阶，回头望去。那是一只褐白相间的斑猫，还没有看见自己，但吉姆还是认为现在下楼太危险了。于是他开启了他漫长的攀登之旅。二楼的楼梯口上有太多的人在走来走去，进进出出不同的房间。被人一脚踩死的概率太大了。一小时后，当他爬到三楼时，正好赶上热火朝天的地毯吸尘作业。他知道许多可怜虫就是这样殒命的，被一头吸入了满是尘埃的湮灭之中。他别无选择，只能继续攀登，直到——可就在这时，突然，在这间阁楼卧室里，他所有的思绪在一部床头电话的刺耳铃声中烟消云散了。虽然他发现自己终于可以挪动四肢中的一肢——一条胳膊了，可他依然一动不动。他担心自己的声音会露馅。就算不会，他又该说什么呢？我不是你们以为的那个人？响了四通铃后，电话沉默了。

他往后一躺，好让他狂跳的心脏平静下来。他练习着挪动双腿。终于，它们动了。但最多只挪了一英寸。他又试着操纵一只胳膊，将它越抬越高，眼看它高高地竖立在头顶。好啦，继续刚才的故事。他奋力爬上最后一级台阶，气喘吁吁地站在顶层楼梯口上。他从离他最近的一道门缝下面钻了进去，进到一套小公寓里。一般情况下，他会直扑厨房，但这次他却攀上了一根床柱，然后拖着精疲力竭的身体，爬到了一只枕头下面。他这一觉睡得真沉，一定睡了——可就在这时，该死，传来了一记敲门声，不等他回应，卧室的房门就开了。一个穿着哔叽色女裤套装的年轻女人站在门槛那里，干脆地点了点头，接着便走了进来。

"我试过给你打电话了，可我想着我最好还是上来一趟。首相，已经快七点半了。"

他不知该如何回答。

那女人（显然是个助理之类的角色）走进屋来，拿起空酒瓶。她的态度未免太随便了些。

"难忘的一夜，我看出来了。"

他不能再这么沉默下去了。他试着从床头发出一声含糊不清的语音，介于呻吟和低语之间。效果不赖。比他想要的更尖一些，带着一点啴啴声，但还算可信。

助理朝那张大桌子打了个手势，指向两只红盒子。"我猜你还没来得及，嗯……"

保险起见，他又祭出了刚才的那个声音，这次音调低了些。

"早饭后，也许你可以花时间……我得提醒你，今天是周三。九点开内阁会。中午是政府要务和首相答问。"

首相答问。他经历过多少场这样的答问会啊：蹲伏在朽烂的护墙板后面，身边围绕着数千名精英同伴，如痴如醉地倾听着会上的发言。反对党领袖咆哮的发问，精彩绝伦、不讲逻辑的答辩，欢闹的冷嘲热讽，恰到好处的学羊叫——这一切他是多么的熟悉啊。能够在这出每周一演的轻歌剧上成为男一号，这可真是梦想成真啊。可他准备得够充分吗？不比任何人差，这是肯定的。瞥一眼那两盒文件就妥了。和他的许多同类一样，他十分向往公文箱。他会脚底抹油，一溜快跑的——虽然他现在只有两只脚。

在他原先挥动着一副漂亮的口器的地方，那块叫人恶心的致密组织动了一下，接着他的第一个人类词语脱口而出：

"好嘞。"

"我会在楼下给你备好咖啡的。"

曾经,他时常在夜深人静之时的茶室地板上啜饮咖啡。咖啡会让他在白天睡不着觉,可他喜欢那滋味,尤其偏爱多加奶的咖啡,再放四块方糖。他心想,这一点他的手下应该都清楚吧。

助理刚一离开房间,他就推开被单,一番努力之后,终于把他那双结节的腿脚晃荡到了地毯上。终于,他站了起来,高得让人眩晕,身子微微摇晃着,一双柔软、苍白的手按着额头,嘴里又开始发出叽里咕噜的声音。几分钟后,当他迈开颤巍巍的步伐朝卫生间走去时,那双手已经开始灵巧地解开睡衣了。他从褪下的衣裤中跨出一步,站上暖洋洋的地热瓷砖。他饶有兴致地把小便滚滚地排入一只特制的瓷钵中,精神也为之一振。可当他转身面对洗脸池上方的镜子时,沮丧再度袭来。一张满是胡茬的椭圆脸盘,摇摇晃晃地撑在一根像是粉色肉茎的粗脖子上,真是让他反胃。那双针孔般的眼睛让他愕然。白里泛黄的两排白牙周围那一圈肿胀膨大、颜色暗沉的皮肉让他恶心。可我来这里，是为了一个崇高的事业，我愿意忍受一切，他自我安慰道，一面看着自己的双手拧开水龙头，伸向修面刷和香皂。

五分钟后，他在铺陈开来的一排衣物前面停下了脚步，身子还在摇晃着，想到要把这些衣服统统穿上身，不由得一阵眩晕。他的同类们对于自己油光水滑的健美身躯很是自豪，绝对不会想要遮遮掩掩。白内裤，黑袜子，蓝白条纹衬衫，深色的西装，黑色的皮鞋。他无动于衷地看着自己的双手用条件反射般的速度系上鞋带，接着回到镜子前面，又用同样的速度打好领带。当他梳理着他姜红色的头发时，一阵乡愁突然袭上心头：他意识到他从前那副亲爱的老甲壳就是这个颜色。至少，我的旧颜还有一处未改的地方——带着这样忧伤的思绪，终于，他站上了楼梯顶。

他开始了令人眩晕的下坡路，相信他的双腿会把他安全地带下楼去，就像他靠着双手修了面，穿了衣服一样。他死死地抓住扶栏，每走一步都要憋住一声呻吟。当他穿过楼梯口，绕过那里的急转弯时，他甚至用两只手抱紧扶栏。他这样子肯定会被人当作是宿醉未醒。可之前他花了一个小时才攀上的楼梯，如今下楼却只用了区区七分钟。在门厅的楼梯下面等待着他的是一群非常年轻的男女，人手一只文件夹。他们毕恭毕敬的低语声——"早安，首相先生"——汇成一曲和风细雨、参差不齐的合唱。他们全都等着他开口，没有人胆敢直视他。

他清了清嗓子，终于开口道："咱们开工吧，好吗？"说完便卡壳了，不知该再怎么往下说，幸好这时一个伙计拨开人群走了过来，一把抓住吉姆的胳膊肘，把他一路推进走廊。这人比其他那些男女都要年长，身上的西装看上去和吉姆自己穿的这件一样价格不菲。

"借步说句话。"

一扇门开了，两人走了进去。"你的咖啡在这里。"

他们来到了内阁室。长桌中间那把最大的椅子前面摆着一只上咖啡的托盘，首相立刻贪婪地扑了上去，最后那几步甚至迫不及待地跑了起来。他想要抢在他的同伴前头，抓紧时间会一会糖缸。可等到他把身子坐进椅子里的时候（几乎顾不上体面了），他的咖啡已经有人在倒了。托盘里没有糖。甚至没有牛奶。不过就在他的杯托投下的那道灰影里，躺着一只垂死的反吐丽蝇，只有他看得见。每过几秒钟它的翅膀就会颤动一下。吉姆费了些劲儿，才一面听着同伴讲话，一面把专注的目光从丽蝇身上别开。他开始觉得自己要打喷嚏了。

"关于1922委员会①。还是那几个该死的老惯犯。"

"啊，是的。"

"昨天晚上。"

"当然。"

丽蝇颤动翅膀的时候，发出几不可闻、表示默许的沙沙声。

---

① 1922委员会，即保守党后座议员委员会，是英国下院的保守党普通议员每周聚会，不受党内高层制约，独立讨论政策的议会团体。该团体对于党魁的人选有着重要的发言权。

"很高兴你不在场。"

一只反吐丽蝇如果死亡超过十分钟，尝起来就会苦涩得离谱。可要是它将死未死或是刚刚咽气，却又别有一番奶酪般的滋味。斯提耳顿干酪，差不离吧。

"是吗？"

"那是一场叛乱。全都登上今早的报纸了。"

真是没办法。首相非打喷嚏不可了。他能感受到它在体内酝酿。也许是因为灰尘太少了吧。他抓紧了椅子。在那爆炸性的一瞬间，他以为自己晕倒了。

"上帝保佑你。听说有人要发起不信任投票。"

当他抬起他那对累赘的眼皮，睁开眼睛时，苍蝇已经不见了。被吹跑了。"妈的。"

"我也有同感。"

"哪儿呢？我是说，这样做的意义在哪儿呢——"

"一如既往。你是一个披着伪装的'顺时派'。不支持'方案'。不是个真正的孤胆侠。推不出一样能通过议会的法案。全无脊梁。诸如此类的话。"

吉姆把杯子连同杯托拖到眼前。没有。他举起不锈钢咖啡壶。下面也没有。

"我和他们一样是'反转派'。"

他的特别顾问——假定这果真是他的身份——沉默不语，似乎是在表达异议。过了一会儿他开口道："我们需要一个计划。现在就要。"

直到这时，他的威尔士口音才显露无遗。威尔士？遥远西部的一个小地方，多山，阴雨连绵，危险莫测。吉姆发现他知道不少事情，各种事情。他知道事情的方式和从前大不一样了。他的认知，就和他的视野一样，是狭隘的。他缺失了与他的全体族类的那种开放、顺时的联结，那片信息素海洋的无限资源。可他终于完整回忆出了指派给他的任务。

"你的建议呢？"

外面有人重重地叩了一记门，接着门便开了，一个高个子男人大步流星地走了进来。此人长着一只大下巴，染黑的头发向后梳着，身穿一件细条纹西装。

"吉姆，西蒙。你俩不介意带上我吧？坏消息。刚刚收到密电，从——"

西蒙打断了他。"本尼迪克特，我俩在密谈。拜托你起开。"

外交大臣面不改色地转过身，走了出去，顺手把门带上，动作小心得近乎夸张。

"这些读私立学校的家伙最让我讨厌的一点就是，"西蒙说，"他们把一切都视作理所当然。当然，你除外。"

"没错。你的计划是什么？"

"你自己也已经说过了。你朝那些死硬分子靠拢一寸，他们只会得寸进尺。你满足了他们的要求，他们反倒往你头上撒泡尿。'方案'的推进一出问题，他们马上怪罪所有人。尤其是怪你。"

"所以呢？"

"公众情绪现在出现了摇摆。民调焦点组的口风变了。

昨晚我们的民调员打电话汇报了结果。我们察觉到了一种普遍的厌倦情绪。一种对于未知的恐惧正在发酵。这些人在担忧他们曾经投票支持的东西,不知道他们亲手放出的是什么。"

"我听说了民调结果。"首相撒谎道。面子很重要。

"重点在这里:我们应该孤立死硬分子。不信任案,吃屎去吧!宣布议会休会几个月。让那些混蛋大吃一惊。或者,还有一个更好的招:改弦更张。倒向——"

"当真?"

"我认真的。你必须倒向——"

"顺时派?"

"对!议会将拜倒在你脚下。你会取得多数的——刚刚好。"

"可人民的意——"

"让他们见鬼去吧。一群屁民,别人说什么就信什么。我们实行的是议会民主制,你才是老大。现在下院瘫了。整个国家在自我分裂。上次有个极端反转派在超市里砍了一个顺时派议员的脑袋。又有一个顺时派小流氓往一个反转派名流头上倒奶昔。"

"骇人听闻，"首相附和道，"他的上衣刚刚洗过呢。"

"这完全是一团糟。吉姆，是时候叫停了。"说完他又压低声音添了一句："你有权力这么做。"

首相直视着顾问的脸，直到现在才将这张脸看了个分明。这是一张狭长的面孔，有着下陷的太阳穴，棕色的小眼睛和一张紧绷的、玫瑰花蕾般的小嘴。他留了一把三天没刮的胡子，脚踩一双休闲鞋，上身里面穿一件超人T恤，外面套一件真丝黑西装。

"你说的这些很有意思。"首相终于开口道。

"我的工作就是保住你的位子，而这是唯一的办法。"

"那将是一个……一个……"吉姆搜肠刮肚地想着那个词。以前，通过信息素，他知道好几种不同的说法。可现在它们都模糊不清了。忽然他想起来了。"一个一百八十度大转弯!"

"不完全是。我把你以前的演讲都过了一遍。里面能找出足够的素材来,让你现在跳船脱身。困难。疑虑。搁置。恰恰是那些死硬分子恨你的地方。雪莉可以帮你先铺好路。"

"真的很有意思,"吉姆站起身来,伸了个懒腰,"我得在开内阁会前亲自和雪莉聊聊。然后我得自己待几分钟。"

他动身绕过长桌,朝门口走去。他渐渐开始从他迈开的大步中感受到某种愉悦,某种全新的掌控感了。尽管他之前根本不敢相信,可只用两只脚的确是能站稳的。离地这么高也几乎不再让他紧张了。现在他很庆幸自己没有当着另一个人的面吞下那只反吐丽蝇。那样做恐怕会让人接受不了。

西蒙答道:"那我就等着听你的想法了。"

吉姆走到门前,伸出一只陌生的手,让手指轻轻地落在门把手上。是的,他能驱动这部柔软的新机器。他缓缓地转过身,享受着这一过程,直到他和自己的顾问面对面——那个男人还没有从椅子上挪身。

"我现在就可以说给你听。我限你半小时内把辞职报告交到我桌子上,并且在十一点钟前离开这栋楼。"

*

新闻秘书雪莉是个温和面善的小不点女人,从头到脚一身黑衣,脸上架着一副超大号的黑框眼镜,活像一只好斗的鹿角甲虫,可谓不甚讨喜。可她和首相倒是很合得来,尽管她往他面前派了一圈报纸,上面的大字标题全都不太友好。"吉姆笨蛋,垃圾桶见!""以上帝的名义,滚蛋吧!"他拾起西蒙的牙慧,管那群坐后座的死硬反转派叫"还是那几个该死的老惯犯",如此一来便给这些新闻蒙上了一层无伤大雅的喜剧色彩。雪莉和吉姆一起咯咯笑了起来。可还有几份相对严肃的报纸一致认为,不信任案很有可能会通过。首相在党内顺时派和反转派之间两头不落好。他太喜欢当和事佬了。他向两派同时伸出橄榄枝,结果得罪了所有人。"在政坛上,"一位知名专栏作家如此写道,"寻求两党合作就意味着死期将至。"人们还普遍认为,即便动议未获通过,发生不信任投票这一事实本身就损害了他的权威。

"我们走着瞧。"吉姆说道。雪莉哈哈大笑,仿佛他刚刚讲了一个超有趣的笑话。

他动身朝门外走去,想要一个人静一静,为下一场会议做好准备。就在他一只脚踩上大街前的那一刻,他指示雪莉把西蒙的辞职信曝给媒体,好堵上记者们的嘴,证明一切正常。对于同事被炒这件事,雪莉没有流露出惊讶之情。相反,她开心地点了点头,一面收起面前的晨报。

对于任何人来说,开内阁会议迟到都是很不得体的做法,但首相除外。等到他走进房间的时候,所有人都已经围着桌子各就各位了。他在财政大臣和外交大臣中间那个属于他的位子上落了座。他紧张吗?谈不上。他只是上紧了弦,蓄势待发,就像一个起跑器上的短跑选手。他的当务之急是显得可信。就像他的手指知道如何打领带一样,首相也知道在他开口说话之前,最好的开场白是沉默不语和用沉稳的目光接触房间里的每一个人。

就在那短短的几秒钟内,当他先后迎上兰开斯特公爵领地大臣特雷弗·哥特、检察总长、下院议长、贸易大臣、交通大臣、不管部大臣的和蔼目光之时——就在那叫人称奇的一瞬间,他立刻认出了他们;一股陌生、超然、心花怒放般的喜悦涌遍他的全身,涌过他的心房,直下他的脊柱。表面上他依然波澜不惊。可他看得一清二楚。几乎他所有的内阁成员都和他有着共同的信念。而比这重要得多得多的是——他也是直到此刻才认识到这一点——他们和他有着同样的来历。当他在那个危机四伏的夜晚一路攀上白厅时,他还以为自己是在单枪匹马执行任务。他万万没有想到,这使命的重担不是他一个人在扛;没想到另一些人和他一样,正直奔内阁各大臣而去,准备占据他们的躯壳,吹起战斗的号角。这二三十位勇士——全民族的一小撮精英——前来接管一个畏缩不前的领导层,来为他们注入勇气。

不过,眼下有一个小问题,一件烦心事,一桩缺憾。他身边有一个叛徒。他只需一瞥便看得分明。乐园里永远藏着一个魔鬼。只有一个。也许他们中有一位勇敢的使者没能从议会大厦抵达终点,而是牺牲在了人类的脚下,倒在了大门外的人行道上,他自己就险些遭此厄运。当吉姆直视外交大臣本尼迪克特·圣约翰的眼眸时,他撞上的是一张人类视网膜,好似一面光秃秃、硬邦邦的墙壁,再也无法前进一步。无法参透。空无一物。只是一个人类。一个冒牌货。一个通敌者。一个人民的敌人。正是那种会参与叛乱,投票颠覆他的政府的人。这个隐患必须解决。时机自会出现。现在不是时候。

但其余的伙伴都到齐了,他一下子便透过他们透明的人类表象认出了他们。一群兄弟姐妹。脱壳变形的一届激进内阁。他们围桌而坐时,并没有透露他们真实的身份,但全都心知肚明。他们的样貌多像人类啊,多么的诡异!可当他直视他们的哺乳纲眼睛,洞穿那不同色泽的灰、绿、蓝,直抵他们闪光的蜚蠊目生命内核时,他的心中便对这群同伴和他们的价值观生出了理解和热爱。那也正是他自己奉行的价值观。钢铁般的勇气和不成功便成仁的意念凝聚着他们。纯洁无瑕、激动人心的理念激励着他们，恰如那"血与土"的信条①。超越了纯粹理性的目标推动着他们，去拥抱一种神秘主义式的民族意识，一种如宗教信仰般简单朴素、纯粹真善的认知。

还有一件事将这群勇士凝聚在了一起，那就是无可避免的贫困与随之而来的泪水——不过，很遗憾，流下那泪水的不会是他们自己。同样无可避免的是，胜利之后，一种深邃高贵的自尊感将赐福普罗大众。此时此刻，这个房间里没有弱者的位置。这个国家即将从可憎的奴役之中解放出来。最优秀的那批人已经开始卸下身上的镣铐了。很快，骑在人民背上的"顺时派"魔鬼就将被叉翻在地。囚笼里总有人面对打开的铁门徘徊不前。让他们继续畏畏缩缩地做选举制的俘

---

① 血与土（Blood and Soil），德文为 Blut und Boden，纳粹主义的核心意识形态之一，宣扬民族的生存倚靠血（民族的血统）与土地（农业生产的基础）。

房，做这个腐败、破产的体制的奴隶吧，他们唯一的慰藉就是民调曲线图和饼分图、乏味的理性，还有他们那可怜的怯懦。他们真应该睁开眼睛看看，一个重大的事件已经脱离了他们的掌控，超越了分析与辩论的范畴，进入了历史。此刻它正在进行中，就在这里，在这张桌边。集体的命运正在内阁那无声而火热的激情中锻造出炉。毫不妥协的反转主义才是主流。开弓没有回头箭！

二

反转主义的起源鲜为人知且争议颇多（仅限于还操心这件事情的那群人中间）。在它问世后的大部分时间里，人们只把它看作是一个思维实验，一个茶余饭后的游戏，一个玩笑。它专属于那些怪人，那些强迫症发作般用绿墨水给报纸不停写信的独狼。那些会在酒吧里把你缠住，烦上你整整一个小时的人。可这个理念一旦为人接受，就会在某些人眼中展现出简约与美好来。只要将货币的流向逆转，整个经济系统，甚至是整个国家，就会得到净化，将一切荒唐、浪费与不公荡涤干净。一周的工作结束后，一位雇员得向公司乖乖交钱，为她许多个小时的辛苦劳作买单。不过，等到她走进商店时，她会因为她拿走的每一样商品而得到慷慨的酬金，金额就以商品的零售价计。法律严禁她中藏现金。在购物中心里奋力血拼了一天后，她存进银行的钱得承受高额负利率的惩罚。在她的储蓄化为乌有之前,她最好是出门找一份更昂贵的工作——或是参加相关的培训。她找到的工作越好——也就是越贵,她就得越努力地去商场血拼,好为这份工作买单。经济因此得到了刺激,有技能的工人也越来越多,人人得益,皆大欢喜。房东得不辞辛劳地采购产品,好付钱给他的房客。政府得兴办核电站,扩展航天计划,好筹资给工人派发税金。酒店经理得置办最上乘的香槟、最柔软的床单、最稀罕的兰花,请来城里头牌乐队里的头牌小号手,这样酒店才有钱付给客人。第二天,在乐池里举办了一场成功的演出后,小号手得走进商场大买特买,这才有钱为他的下一场演出买单。最终的结果就是充分就业。

十七世纪的两位重要的经济学家——约瑟夫·芒和乔塞亚·蔡尔德——曾经轻描淡写地提到过金钱的逆向流通,但草草就将这个想法打发,没有给予它多少关注。至少,我们知道这个理论在当时就有传播。亚当·斯密的《国富论》对此只字未提,马尔萨斯和马克思也是一样。到了十九世纪晚期，美国经济学家弗朗西斯·阿马萨·沃克对于改变货币的流向表露过些许兴趣，但那显然只是在口头交流中，而非在他的众多著作中。1944年，在那场构建了战后经济秩序、创立了国际货币基金组织的关键性会议——布莱顿森林会议上，巴拉圭代表赫苏斯·X.贝拉斯克斯在大会下属的一个小组委员会上发表了一通热情洋溢的呼吁，他的发言被完整录入了会议纪要。他没有争取到支持者，但这位代表被公认为公开使用这一术语的第一人。

在西欧，这一理念时不时地会吸引到一些右翼或极右团体，因为它似乎能够限制国家权力与权限。在英国，比方说，尽管最高一级的所得税率依然是百分之八十三，但如此一来政府就得向最奋不顾身的那批购物狂派发几十亿英镑了。据传，基思·约瑟夫曾试图勾起玛格丽特·撒切尔对于"反向流通经济学"的兴趣，可她没有时间听这个，在1980年4月的一次BBC访谈中，基思爵士坚称这样的传闻纯属无中生有。在整个九十年代，直到二十一世纪头十年，反转主义只是在各个私人讨论小组和不甚知名的中右翼智库中保持着某种低调的存在。

等到反转主义党挟其民粹、反精英的口号闪亮登场时，许多人已经对其"反向流通"的理论耳熟能详了，哪怕是在它的反对者中间。而在反转主义者们争取到了美国总统阿尔奇·特普的背书后，尤其是在这一主张开始分流选民的投票后，作为回应，保守党开始缓慢地右倾化甚至是极右化。但对于保守党主流而言，反转主义仍然是——借用前财政大臣乔治·奥斯本的话来说——"世界上最愚蠢的想法"。没人知道究竟是哪个经济学家抑或是记者发明了"顺时派"这个词来指代那些希望货币按久经考验的老办法继续流通的人。许多人都声称自己是第一个。

而在左翼阵营，尤其是在"老左派"当中，总有一小撮人对反转主义格外宽容。其中的一个缘由是，他们相信这种理论能赋予失业者以权力。既不需要为工作买单，又有大把的时间来购物，这些人完全可以大发横财——就算那财富不能表现为囤积的钞票,也可以体现在拥有的商品中。与此同时,家大业大的富人却没法利用自己的财富,除了把钱花在创造利润丰厚的工作机会上。而当工人阶级的工党选民意识到将儿子送进伊顿公学或是将女儿送进切尔滕纳姆女子学院能够给他们带来怎样的收入后,他们也开始提升抱负,转而投向反转主义的旗下了。

为了稳住自己的选民支持率,安抚党内的反转派,保守党在2015年的竞选宣言中承诺将就逆转货币流向这一动议举行全民公投。最终的结果出人意料,这在很大程度上要归因于工薪阶层中的穷人和所有阶层中的老人结成了一个秘而不宣的联盟。前者在现状下一无所有也无所顾忌,而且他们还盼望着把必需品和奢侈品一起拿回家,盼望着做一回手头有钱的富人,不管是多么昙花一现。而老人呢,出于认知能力的衰退,把反转主义理解成了一项让时光倒流的提议,从而在怀旧情愫的驱使下被其所吸引。这两个群体——穷人和老人——都在不同程度上受到了民族主义狂热的鼓动。凭借着一个神来之笔，反转主义媒体成功地将他们的事业包装成了一项爱国主义义务，一个民族复兴与净化的承诺：这个国家的一切错误，从财富与机遇的不公到南北对立再到工资水平的停滞，都是由金融流向造成的。如果你热爱你的祖国和人民，你就应该颠覆现有的秩序。过去的货币流向只符合蔑视大众的统治精英的利益。"让钱倒流"成为了许多直击人心的口号中的一句。

举行了公投的那位首相事后立刻就辞职了，自此销声匿迹。取而代之的是一位折衷妥协的候补者——半心半意的顺时派詹姆斯·山姆斯。刚刚去白金汉宫觐见过女王之后，他就在唐宁街的台阶上承诺将尊重人民的意愿。钱会倒流的。但是，正如许多经济学家和另一些评论员在部分发行量很小的报纸以及无人关注的专业期刊上预测的那样，这不是一件容易的事。第一个压倒一切的问题关系到海外贸易。德国人一定会开开心心地把我们的货物连同我们丰厚的货款一起收下。但他们一定不会出于礼尚往来就在他们出口给我们的汽车里面塞满钞票。面对这样的贸易赤字，我们很快就会破产的。

所以，一个反转主义经济体怎样才能在一个顺时主义世界中繁荣发展呢？与我们最重要的贸易伙伴——欧洲人的谈判陷入了僵局。三年过去了。一个主体是顺时派的议会一头要面对常识，一头要服从人民的意愿，真是左右为难，拿不出任何实际的解决方案。山姆斯继承了一个占微弱优势的多数党，却在政党内部各个狂热的派别间拼命挣扎。尽管如此，一些新闻报纸依然称他为"幸运吉姆"，因为情况完全可以比这更糟：反对派领袖霍勒斯·克雷布本人正是一名后列宁主义左派的老年反转主义者。

就在山姆斯犹豫不决，他的内阁也因为路线不同而继续四分五裂之时，保守党后座议员中一个纯粹主义团体的立场开始变得愈发强硬。英国必须孤军奋战，然后凭借自己的榜样让全世界追随我们。如果世界拒绝追随我们，那么错的是这个世界。这就是ROC。一国反转主义（Reversalism in One Country）。接着是铺天盖地的歌声和涂鸦——争分夺秒ROC。我们以前就孤军奋战过，在1940年，法国沦陷后，那时纳粹德国的恐怖统治席卷了欧洲。如今干吗还非要买他们的汽车不可呢？可山姆斯退缩了，忙着向各派势力许下各种承诺。大部分经济学家、《城市杂志》记者、商业领袖以及整个金融界全都预测，如果山姆斯跟着强硬反转派的路线走，将会有一场经济灾难。银行、清算所、保险经纪人还有跨国公司已经开始向海外转移了。知名科学家和诺贝尔奖得主纷纷在报纸上刊登绝望的公开信。可是在街头，民众的呼喊气壮山河、发自内心：卷起袖子干！社会上滋长着一股愤怒的情绪，一种感觉受到背叛的合理怀疑。一幅报纸漫画将吉姆·山姆斯描绘成莎翁笔下的格洛斯特伯爵，瞎了眼，摇摇晃晃地站在白垩悬崖边，而埃德加——一个强硬的"约翰牛"反转派——正催促他跳下去。

就在这时，没有任何预兆，出乎所有人预料，山姆斯和他那届犹豫不决的内阁似乎找到了勇气。他们准备好跳崖了。

*

首相一一审视了围着桌子的那一双双眼睛,确信自己不会突然放声高唱欢快的信息素之歌后,便立刻说了几句严肃的欢迎辞。他的声音低沉冷静。他的右颧骨上方的一块肌肉不停地抽动着。这一幕过去从来没有人见到过。在他的开场白中,他只轻描淡写地提到了一回他们共同的身份——他说这是一届"新"内阁,从今往后在议会投票中将团结如一人。不许再有人破坏纪律。只有盲目的集体服从。他话音刚落,桌子周围就响起了一阵经久不息、表示赞同的沙沙声和嗯嗯声。他们的思想统一了,他们是一个为了目标甘愿献身的虫群。

接下来就该谈正事了。走出这扇门,他们会看到近期的一项选民态度调查报告,报告打印了许多份,他们应该各拿一份,好好读一读。他们会注意到其中一项数据:二十五岁到三十五岁的年龄组中,有三分之二的人期盼一个"不必在乎议会"的强人领袖。

"眼下,我们还得在乎,"吉姆说,"不过……"他让后半句话悬在了半空中,房间里顿时静悄悄的。他继续往下说道:"被一拖再拖的反转法案将在三个月内重回下院。所有的反对派修正案都将被投票否决。适应措施现在就要启动。我们将在过渡举措上投入八十亿,财政大臣可以确认这一点。"

财政大臣是一个冷冰冰的小个子,长着一双灰白的眉毛和一把白花花的山羊胡。他克制住片刻的惊诧,道貌岸然地点了点头。

首相也点头回应,给了他一个克制的微笑,双唇紧闭,笑不露齿。这是至高的奖赏。"现在该让你们知道了。我已经把'反转日'——R日——定在了12月25日,这一天商店全都关门了。R日之后的圣诞季销售额对GDP会是一个巨大的提振。"

他环顾四周。他们全都用专注的目光望着他。没有一个人在会场提供的笔记本上信手涂鸦。吉姆举起双臂，十指交叉抵住后脑勺，感受到了一种非同寻常的愉悦。

"我们将按部就班地实现量化宽松，印发钞票，好让百货商店有钱为消费者买单，而消费者也有钱为自己的工作买单。"

外交大臣突然插话了。"有一处局势正在发展，就在——"

首相几不可察地摇了摇头，让他闭嘴。他让双臂落回体侧。"实现R日——我们倒不如就叫它'我们的日子'——是我们无可逃避的第一要务。可我们的第二要务几乎同等重要。没有它，第一要务很可能失败。"

他停顿了一下，好加强语言效果。就在那短暂的间歇，他抓紧时间思考了一下该如何对付本尼迪克特·圣约翰。一个另类。唐宁街不是能轻易安排一场完美谋杀的地方。很久以前，那个顶着黑色大礼帽装腔作势的笨蛋杰里米·索普[①]

[①] 杰里米·索普（1929—2014），英国政治家，自由党领袖，曾因唆使谋杀其同性恋情人以掩盖政治丑闻未遂而受审。

倒是在下院谋划过一次这样的行动。他的惨败足以警醒后人了。

"前方的路上会有一些坎坷,我们必须让人民和我们同行。恰恰就在我们需要狂热的民意支持的时候,焦点组的情绪出现了躁动。这极度重要。所以,我们要给低收入人群加税,给富裕人群减税。25号之后给工人们派发大礼包。而为了给这一行动买单——我相信我们睿智的财政大臣一定会同意的——我们将再雇用两万名警察、五万名护士、一万五千名医生和能够确保垃圾日日收的二十万名垃圾工,以此提升财政收入。在减税政策的帮助下,这些新雇员应该能够轻易为自己的工作买单。况且中国人在建的那三个核电站项目还欠我们八千亿。"

房间里那专注的沉默氛围似乎松动了,品质降级了。没人相信中国政府。他们会付钱吗?他们会把他们那庞大的经济体反转过来吗?有人礼貌地咳嗽了一声。一些人在查看自己的指甲。就算他还没有失去内阁的支持,吉姆意识到他也只差一步就要引来阁员们的怀疑了。替他解围的是交通大臣——来自东北部选区的一个叼着烟斗、和蔼面善的议员,大家都认为此人野心勃勃。

"我们应该继续推进连通伯明翰的高铁线,这样就能省下一大笔钱。"

"非常好。谢谢你,简。"

一身肌肉、挺着方下巴的国防大臣汉弗莱·巴顿受到了鼓舞,也开口说道:"还应该再扩编四艘航母。"

"棒极了,汉弗。"

"新增一万个监狱空位可以带来二十五亿收入。"

"赞,弗兰克。"

突然间,他们全都一拥而上,急着要讨欢心,你争我抢地嚷嚷着这一新制度为之亮起绿灯的各种部门项目。

首相往椅背上一靠,满面春风;他没有去细听那些人在说些什么,只是偶尔咕哝一句:"真不错……要的就是这股劲头……顶呱呱!"

057

不可避免地，过了一阵子，一股倦怠的情绪降临在了会场上，就在这一时的沉寂中，外交大臣说话了。

"那我们怎么办？"

所有的脑袋都恭敬地转向了本尼迪克特·圣约翰。就在那一刻，吉姆意识到了只有他了解这个男人的特殊身份。

"什么？"

外交大臣两手一摊，表示问题显而易见。"就拿我来说吧。但其实你也一样。明年我要代表英国跑遍全世界各个国家的首都，劝说各国政府加入我们。而我的年薪是十四万一千四百零五英镑。"

"那又怎样？"

"我的家庭责任如此沉重，这样的生活费实在是太高了啊。我上哪儿去找时间购这么多的物来为我的工作买单呢？"

又一次，桌子底下响起了轻轻的沙沙声。吉姆环顾四周。本尼迪克特是在冷嘲热讽吗？也许他是在为房间里的所有人代言。

首相用充满鄙视的目光瞪着他。"该死,我该怎么……你只要,嗯……"

又一次,交通大臣简·菲什向他伸出了援手。

"上亚马逊,本尼。点一下鼠标。给你自己提辆特斯拉!"

这一优雅的解决方案引得所有人长舒了一口气。首相准备讨论下一个问题了,可圣约翰还没完。

"我很担心。英镑很可能会在你的R日受到重挫。"

你的?这不可容忍,但首相还是挤出了一个慈祥的表情。"那有利于我们的进口。"

"这正是我要说的。出口。我们得把更多的资金转出海外。"

吉姆就像在跟一个小孩说话那样解释道:"我们的进口收入会平衡这一开支的。"

"在未来三年中,我们能够争取到的唯一伙伴就是圣基茨和尼维斯联邦。吉姆,后果会是毁灭性的。"

每一位大臣都密切观察着这场正面挑战。首相突然爆发出的爽朗大笑是发自内心的,因为他已经看到了未来——不但看到了外交大臣的神秘死亡,还看到了他的葬礼,一个次高规格的活动,吉姆本人将到场致辞。圣保罗大教堂。埃尔加的《宁录》。皇家骑兵卫队。想到这里他记起来了:他还没有吃早饭。

"哎,本尼迪克特呀,卡尔·马克思曾经说过,一个国家能承受相当多的毁灭。"

"是亚当·斯密说的。"

"那么这话就更有道理了。"

大臣们全都放松了下来。他们很乐意把这最后一句话看作是一锤定音,一语定调。吉姆喘了口气,打算宣布下一项举措。

可外交大臣继续说道:"现在该讨论那件大事了。"

"上帝啊,伙计。"内政大臣弗兰克·科德愤愤地说。

本尼迪克特的位子正对着国防大臣。两人交换了一个眼神,巴顿耸耸肩,低头看着手。你来告诉他们吧。

"局势尚在发展中。目前还没有官方声明。但有人告诉我,《每日邮报》正要把这件事登上网站。所以你们也全都应该知道。我通常不会——"

"有话快讲。"吉姆说。

"今天早上七点刚过,一艘法国护卫舰与我们的一条捕鱼船'拉金'号在布列塔尼近海处相撞,距罗斯科夫不远。船撞成了两截。上面有六人。全都从水里拖上来了。"

"太好了。那我们就——"

"全淹死了。"

在首相和他的同僚们的成长过程中,死亡是一种家常便饭,按照习俗死者身故后其他人要大快朵颐,这既是一种必要的卫生措施,又是一种相当不错的——他赶忙掐断了思绪。他老练地先沉默了一小会儿,然后才开口说道:"一场悲剧。可海上总有意外发生。我们干吗要讨论这个?"

"那条渔船在非法捕捞。在法国领海上。"

"那又怎样?"

外交大臣把下巴枕在两只手上。"我们一面对这件事保密,一面通知了死者家人。可事情在推特上传开了。现在网上流传的故事是,法国人蓄意撞沉了我们的船。强力伸张他们的主权。"

兰开斯特公爵领地大臣问道:"法国人怎么说?"

"大雾天,小木船,距海岸线两公里远,发射机应答器不知怎的出了问题。渔船没有出现在护卫舰的雷达上。我们自己的海军数据和其他的信息源全都佐证了法国人的说法。"

"这么说,事情就很清楚了。"检察总长说道。

外交大臣看了眼手表。"《邮报》今天上午要在他们的网站上登一篇气势汹汹的文章。煽动爱国主义愤怒。很快他们的故事就会传遍各个平台。事态在恶化。五十分钟前,就在我们刚刚坐下的时候,有人朝法国大使馆扔了一块砖头,砸破了大使馆的一扇窗户。"

他停顿了一下,看着首相。"我们需要一份来自最高层的声明。给这场胡闹降降温。"

他们全都看着吉姆。吉姆仰面靠在椅背上，对着天花板说了句："嗯。"

本尼迪克特拿出连哄带劝的语气继续说道："再给法国总统打一个电话，把通话记录下来，如何？"

"嗯。"

所有人都看着，等待着。

终于，他扶正椅子，朝着内阁秘书点了点头，后者按照惯例坐在一个较远的位子上。"如果他们要一起下葬，葬礼我要去。"

外交大臣忙不迭地说："那样做似乎有点——"

"等等。我还有个更好的主意。如果七具棺材能一起运回来——你们最好确保它们一起运回来——我打算到场迎接——码头上，飞机场，管它是在哪儿。"

其他人全都呆若木鸡，与其说是被他给气傻了，不如说是被他迷住了；外交大臣的身子则在发抖。他眼看着就要站起来了，却又坐回了位子上。"吉姆。你不能这么干。"

首相突然间一脸的春风得意。他换上了一副风趣活泼、冷嘲热讽、忽上忽下的语调。"我说，本尼迪克特，等会儿散会以后，我要你拐个弯，回你漂亮的办公室，然后做两件事情。你得召见法国大使，要求他做出解释。然后你得把你的所作所为告诉你的新闻办公室。"

外交大臣深吸一口气。"我们不能玩游戏。法国是我们的一个非常亲密的盟友。"

"我们的六位勇士死了。在有人能够证明事情并非如此之前，我只能假定这是一场可鄙的攻击事件。"

终于，国防大臣鼓起了勇气。他的嗓音听起来像是被人掐住了脖子一样。"事实上，海军部的数据相当可靠。"

"海军部！一群趋炎附势之徒，个个都是。毫无疑问，他们都有买在多尔多涅①的农庄要考虑。"

这话说得好。那真是法国一个讨人嫌的英国角。他们

---

① 多尔多涅省，位于法国东北部，其英国侨民的数量在法国首屈一指。

全都围着桌子咯咯笑着。圣约翰的下巴那绷紧的线条表示他没有什么要说的了。可首相依然狠狠地盯着他,盯了差不多有半分钟。这眼神的效果可谓杀鸡儆猴,尤其是反应在汉弗莱·巴顿身上——此人因为在伞兵团第二营当过上尉而在国内颇有人气。此刻他对桌子上摆在面前的那只水杯发生了浓厚的兴趣。他用两只手紧紧地握住杯子。

"我们会让美国人站在我们这边的,"吉姆说,"他们对于法国人有着特殊的感情。有意见吗?很好。现在,下一个议题。"他从口袋里掏出一张废纸,是从《观察者》杂志上撕下来的一页。纸片上面用铅笔拟了一份清单。"为了庆祝R日,我们要铸造一款十英镑的纪念币。我的构想是印上钟面的镜像。"

"妙啊……绝妙的构想。"大家异口同声地说道。财务大臣用力吞了一口唾沫,点了点头。这时有人说:"印在反面,我猜。"

首相怒目四顾,寻找作乱者。这个玩笑彻底失败了。

"还有别的想法吗？"

没有了。

"下一个。我们要设立一个R日国定假。圣诞季显然不行，所以我打算选一个来年最近的日子——1月2日。有意见吗？"

"没有。"他们咕哝道。

"很好。那一天碰巧是我的生日。"

一听这话，全体内阁都拍着桌子向他致敬，外交大臣除外。

首相谦逊地举起一只手示意克制，屋子里立刻安静了下来。在他短暂的前世中，他从未体验过这样的满足感。他忽然觉得，从他苏醒的那一刻直到现在，已经过去了整整五年，而不是三四个钟头——那时的他悲伤又疯狂，无力控制四肢，甚至连舌头都动不了。他从同僚们的脸上看到了这一点：他说了算，他举足轻重，不管是在这里还是在这个国家里，甚至是在国外。难以置信。激动人心。妙不可言。什么也挡不住他。

他瞥了一眼清单下面的内容。"啊,没错。我有了个想法。反转主义运动需要一首歌,一首正能量的歌。有点像是颂歌。比《欢乐颂》要时髦一点儿。然后我想起来了。这首六十年代的流行歌。《走回幸福》。你们肯定知道这首歌的。不知道?上帝啊,海伦·夏皮罗!"

他们不知道这首歌,也不知道她。可他们不敢摇头。不管是什么在暗中凝聚着他们,他们现在都完全入戏了,沉浸在他们各自的角色中。他们无知的代价是高昂的,因为首相开始用颤抖的男中音唱了起来,双臂大张,面部僵硬地咧嘴笑着,像一个职业低吟歌手。

"走回幸福,唔啪—哦—耶—耶。"

他们也不敢看彼此的眼睛。他们意识到一个错误的微笑可以终结他们的职业生涯。当首相扭扭手指,示意一起来的时候,他们也不敢不加入合唱。他们庄严地齐声唱起了"耶—耶—耶—巴—当—毕—多",仿佛他们唱的是休伯特·帕里①的颂歌。

即便是在放声高歌的时候,吉姆也看到了外交大臣嘴巴紧闭。甚至都没有假唱。他两眼瞪着前方,一动不动,也许是因为尴尬。或者是鄙夷?

就在合唱草草收尾的时候,圣约翰站了起来,不知道是在对谁说话:"唔,我还有事情要做,你们知道的。"他没有对首相打招呼,就匆匆离开了房间。

吉姆扭头目送他离开的时候,惊诧地意识到这般愉悦竟可以同这般仇恨在心中同时并存。人类的心真是一件奇妙的物什,而现在这颗心已经完全由他掌控了。

*

吉姆宣布散会以后,花了几分钟时间独处,准备他的要务声明。他选了几句语录交给雪莉,让她加工成一篇新闻

---

① 休伯特·帕里(1848—1918),英国作曲家,其颂歌《耶路撒冷》在英国被誉为第二国歌。

稿。她的活儿干得又快又好。等到来人通知他轿车正等在外头，大门为他敞开的时候，媒体已经得到了风声：一股大胆的新风正席卷他的政府。迈出大门，步入日光，高高地凌驾于他昨晚爬过的那道门槛——这感觉真是好极了。听着对街的人们兴奋地冲他叽里哇啦地嚷嚷着各种问题，这感觉同样好极了。大门在他身后关上了，他在门外驻足了片刻，给了摄影师们那必要的半分钟，但他没有说话。他只是举起一只手，友好地向人们致意，给了摄像头一丝坚定的淡淡笑容。他现在已经能完全掌控他那双目并用、非马赛克式的多彩聚焦视线了，他让这视线慢慢地扫过记者们的脸，扫过镜头；然后，就在捷豹XJ Sentinel（一款很合他口味的防弹车）缓缓停下，打开车门时，他以胜利的姿态举起双手，咧开大嘴笑着，然后弯腰溜进了后座。

在从白厅到议会大厦的短暂车程上，他得空品味了一下那将要到来的一刻：他会站在公文箱边，清楚无误地表明他麾下政府的意图。想到蹲伏在护墙板后面的那群无影又无声的听众时,他心绪难平。此时此刻他们应该就已经在黑暗中聚集了。他的家人该多么为他自豪啊。

*

摘自议会议事录,9月19日,卷663政府要务

首相(詹姆斯·山姆斯)

如您准许,议长先生,我将就政府的任务发表声明——事实上,这是一届全新的保守党政府。当议案回到本议院的时候,议长先生,我们的任务将是实现反转主义,为的是团结我们伟大的国家,重新为她注入活力,不但要使她再次伟大,还要使她成为地球上最伟大的地方。等到2050年,英国很有可能——不是不可能——成为欧洲最伟大、最繁荣的经济体。我们将是一个全新的反向流通贸易协定网的中心。在所有领域,我们都将成为这颗星球上的冠军。我们将成为电动飞机的地球家园。我们将引领世界,保护我们宝贵的星

球免遭摧残。这个世界还将追随我们光辉的榜样，每一个国家都将争先恐后地逆转货币流向——【被喧哗声打断】

议长先生

肃静。议院里太嘈杂了。太多的议员自以为冲着首相大呼小叫个人意见没什么不对。我们来澄清一下：这就是不对。

首相

议长先生，我为您的介入喝彩。本届政府不再有分歧。我本人和所有的内阁成员已合为一体，我们用一个意念说话。我们的团结可敬可畏。议案因而必将通过。没有什么能阻挡我们。我们将使行政部门的运转进入涡轮增压状态，来为过渡期做好准备。我们将迅速行动，加速我们的贸易协议，并使其拓展到勇敢的圣基茨和尼维斯联邦之外的地区。在那之前，我们宣布实行"一国反转主义"。我们将孤军奋战，正如我们曾经孤军奋战过的那样。许多关于反转主义的负面情绪已经过火得离谱了。现在不是沉溺于软弱的顺时派思维的时候。每一个人都不该再对这件事有一丝怀疑：货币流通就要转向了——而且转得正是时候。在第一天，在 R 日，宏观和微观层面都将感受到反转的正面效果。在 R 日，譬如说，我们得到新授权的警官也许会截停一辆危险超速的汽车，然后透过窗户递进去两张五十英镑的钞票。面对可能的刑事指控，那个驾驶员便有责任用这笔钱加班工作并为加班时间买单，或者是找一份稍微好一点的工作。这只是一个例子，议长先生，但说明的是反转主义将如何刺激经济，为我们杰出的国民提供激励机制，并使我们的民主制度更加强健。

反转主义还将赐福我们的未来——清洁、绿色、繁荣、团结、充满自信又雄心勃勃。当我们齐心协力，鼓足干劲，共赴使命时，顺时经济学的流毒连同它那推行扼杀进取精神的规章制度、给健康与安全制造障碍的官僚主义大山将从我们的头上被铲除——我们所有人，一个接着一个。很快，它还将从地球上所有的国家头上被铲除。我们站在一个黄金时代的起点。议长先生，我将这个未来托付给本院，正如我将这份声明托付给你们。

几位议员阁下起立——

议长先生

肃静。

【待续】

三

那天早上朝法国大使馆扔砖头的那个年轻人逃跑了,警方没有逮捕任何人。这件事巴黎注意到了。事件发生的时候,聚集在骑士桥的群众人数估计在五十人上下。到了傍晚,人数已经上升到了五百多,其中一些是坐着反转主义党安排的巴士从赫尔港一路赶来的渔民。人群又是唱歌又是叫嚷,但除此以外这还算是一场和平的示威。当局增调过来的五名警员无事可做,只能站在大使馆的正门边上看戏。可四点半刚过,就有人扔了"一枚燃烧装置"。那东西有惊无险地落在了一扇窗户下面几棵月桂树旁的湿草地上,没有引燃。那是一只牛奶瓶,里面装了差不多一英寸高的打火机油。相关报道称其为汽油弹,严格说来这么讲或许没有错。这起袭击巴黎也注意到了。

那天下午的早些时候,法国大使亨利·德·克莱蒙·莱罗伯爵被召进外交和联邦事务部解释那六位英国渔民之死。据官方描述，这次会面是"富有建设性的"，大使向遇难者家属衷心表达诚挚的哀悼，同时对这起意外的悲剧致以最深切的歉意。这一切媒体几乎没怎么注意到，因为下午五点首相从唐宁街现身的时候，发表了一篇很不寻常的强硬声明。那枚所谓的炸弹，尽管应受谴责，却在经过检视后被发现只是一只爆竹——事实上，是"一枚受潮的哑炮"，很可能不过是一个非常没品味的玩笑。接着山姆斯高声念出了六名死难者的名字，称他们为"英国英雄"。他同样向痛失亲人的家属表达了最深切的哀悼，还说他对这起悲剧事件"深感不安"，而法国大使早先给出的解释"并不完全令人满意"。首相已经听取了专家的意见。以现代技术的水平，尤其是一艘新锐海军舰艇的技术水平，很难理解一条身长三十英尺的渔船怎么会在雾气中探测不到，不管那雾气有多大。他认为渔船的船长可能不知道自己身处法国领海，正在非法捕捞。山姆斯承认在一个建立于规则之上的国际秩序中，领土主权必须得到尊重。然而——说到这儿他停顿了一下——当侵犯主权的行为发生时,"反应必须慎重而适当"。因此,他正在"寻求我们非常要好的朋友——法国人更进一步的澄清"。他拒绝了提问,匆匆转身钻回了唐宁街10号。

顷刻间,一场外交危机从悲剧之中诞生了。拉鲁塞总统本来就已经被"英国反转"及其威胁到法国对英国的红酒与奶酪出口搞得既困惑又恼火了;如今,用他的发言人的话来说,英国人居然"怀疑一位非常要好的朋友的话"让他"感到失望"。山姆斯当局居然暗示"谋杀误入我们的近海水域的无辜渔民"是法国政府的政策,"这是在公然侮辱法国所珍视的一切价值"。很显然,在一个使国家陷入分裂的决定所引发的困局中,山姆斯先生是为"一场非理性的推特风暴所人为煽动助长的怒火燎原而成的一阵民族主义狂飙"在幕后撑腰。虽然很不情愿,但总统还是决定召回大使。亨利·德·克莱蒙·莱罗伯爵将返回巴黎商讨对策。

如此,吉姆也就有了足够的理由决定召回英国驻巴黎大使。事情发展得很好。在这样一个困难时期，国家需要一个坚定的敌人。爱国记者们赞扬首相从气势上压倒了法国人，为"我们牺牲的小伙子们"说话。他在下院发表的要务声明同样在一些重要的报刊版块上颇受好评。《每日邮报》上的一篇评论文章就起了这样的大字标题："是谁点燃了吉姆胸中的那团火？"

忙碌的第一天收尾后，首相退回了自己在楼顶的那个小套间，忙着弄懂推特——他认定，这就是信息素潜意识的一个原始版本。他读了阿尔奇·特普的最新推文，开始怀疑美国总统是——仅仅是有这个可能——"我们中的一员"。白厅IT小组派来的一个一脸谄媚的家伙帮助首相开了自己的账号。不到两小时，他就有了十五万名追随者。又过了一小时，这个数字翻了一番。

就在吉姆放开腿脚躺在沙发上的时候，他发现，想要以岸然的姿态指摘罗斯科夫事件（现在人们都这么叫了），推特是一个完美的媒介。他的第一次尝试既无力又缺乏创意。

"顺时派拉鲁塞就是个撸瑟（loser）；在我看来他是我们记得的法国总统中最没有能力的一个。"在我看来——好像还有别人似的。真水。可覆水难收了。第二天，美国总统早早就醒了，在自己的床头引领了这场争论，好好示范了一回该怎么发推。"小不点希尔维·拉鲁塞打沉了几艘英国舰船。**真糟糕！**"这是一首诗，将高密度的语意与摆脱细节的灵巧轻盈天衣无缝地结合起来。拉鲁塞被他以一个嘲弄先是去雄化，然后被贬损；而不管这句嘲弄是真是假（他的名字是西尔万①，他身高一米七五），都必将成为他永远的标签；那条渔船变成了一艘舰船，然后一艘舰船变成了几艘舰船；他没有啰里啰唆地去提死者。最终的判决既童真又纯粹，既过目难忘又是一个完全正确的单音节词。还有最后那几个大写字母，像是一个夸张的谢幕礼，还有那个言简意赅的惊叹号！这真是传授如何让想象力自由驰骋的一节课，来自那片自由

---

① 希尔维（Sylvie）是女性的名字，西尔万（Sylvain）则是男子名。

人的土地。

晚些时候，吉姆手握铅笔面对笔记本，考虑要对反转法案做些改进。他看到了罪犯能从这里头钻到空子。丢掉工作，不要命地买东西，往皮箱里塞满现金，跳船逃亡国外，逃到某个肮脏的欧盟经济体，再开一个银行账户。去法国加来打工挣钱，再来英国多佛血拼挣钱。混账。解决方案再清楚不过了——反正这件事原本也要做。无现金社会将为每个人在商店里挣到的每一英镑和花在工作上的每一英镑创立一串数码足迹。私藏超过二十五英镑的现金将是刑事犯罪行为，对此要广而告之。最高量刑？最好不要太严厉，一开始不要。那么，五年吧。

他用工整的手写体飞快地写着笔记，享受着让字母在笔下成形的过程。大拇指和其他四指相对——这主意倒还不坏。智人这种年轻的暴发户物种偶尔会拿出一个有用的创意来。至于思想的阐述或传播——书写，尽管有着手艺上的魅力，却是一种叫人伤心的模拟数据。他奋笔疾书的过程中只停下来一回，狼吞虎咽了一碟用托盘送到他面前的帕尔马干酪。沙拉他则碰都没碰。

下一件事。议案一获通过，他的首要考量当然是说服美国人将他们的经济反转过来。这件事办成了，一切就都顺理成章了。中国人要为他们的出口买单，也就只能实行反转；日本人和欧洲人也一样。拉特普入伙需要事先策划，好好招待。吉姆的笔记写到第四张纸了。问题：阿·特不喝酒/用国事访问软化/和女王陛下晚宴 金马车 号衣男仆 鼓号齐鸣 议会演讲 等等等等/最高等级的嘉德勋位外加维多利亚十字勋章外加荣誉爵士/怀特俱乐部会员/送他海德公园作私人高尔夫球场。

可美国总统是一个严肃的人，品味很不简单，有着他自己的道德自信，他的成长背景也没有教会他认识荣誉体系中那些绶带勋章的精妙魅力。对于一个拥有更昂贵的俱乐部、更大的高尔夫球场的人来说，怀特俱乐部和海德公园算得了什么呢？当一个人一辈子都会是"总统先生"时，谁还会在乎"爵士"头衔呢？那天下午晚些时候，首相认真思考了一会儿这个问题。他已经指派手下好好调研了美国司法体系的某些微妙细节、总统的权限，以及这二者在一个反转经济体中会有怎样的境遇。对于美国宪法第二条，吉姆现在掌握了他所需要知道的一切。他认识到了法律的力量和总统行政命令的惊人权限。和大多数人一样，他早就知道总统是美国三军总司令。内阁办公室为他提供了一份美国国防预算从协商到生效的流程概览。他在笔记本里记下了未来数年的精确预算数字，以十亿美元计。检察总长已经来过唐宁街，向他解释了形势。美国总统只要自己下令，就可以将国会同意的国防预算下放给他自己的办公室。按照标准的反转流程，资金会在系统中一路向上回流，从陆军、海军与空军人员，以及他们所有的供应商与所有的生产商那里，直接流转到总统手中。七千一百六十亿美元就全是他的了。

"他个人的？合法合规的？"吉姆问检察总长。

"是的，合法合规的。这会开创一个让他的对手们大吃一惊的先例。不过就这位总统而言,人们已经习惯于大吃一惊了。"

"让我把话说清楚了,"吉姆说,"他可以把这笔钱存进银行?"

"当然了。开曼群岛,也许吧。俄国总统应该可以帮忙。就算利率再低,他也可以靠吃七十亿或八十亿一年的利息过得还不错,甚至都不用碰本金。"

"那美国的国防怎么办?"

检察总长哈哈大笑。"国会再批预算呀。如今,他们可喜欢借钱了。"

然而此刻,就在街道那头的大本钟哀伤地敲响十一点整时,吉姆开始焦虑他该怎么在电话里推销这件事。特普可不喜欢简朴的生活。七千一百六十亿够吗?他该不该建议总统把教育预算也私存了?还有医保预算?可那需要三道行政命令。太复杂了。他只能碰碰运气了。现在是华盛顿时间下午六点。总统应该在忙着看电视,可能不希望被打扰。吉姆瞪着他那只空空的晚餐盘,目不转睛地看着上面那结了硬壳的色彩漩涡,这里一道紫红,那里一片奶白。又犹豫了几秒钟后,他拨了楼下夜班岗的电话,叫他们安排一次不留记录的通话。他们花了二十五分钟的时间交换身份识别协议,启动人声扰频加密,唤起总统的注意,然后又花了十分钟才和他连上线。鉴于这是一次没有预先安排的通话,这速度算是不错了。

"吉姆。"

"总统先生。希望我没有打断你的某场重要的——"

"没有,只是,嗯……我听说你跟法国人杠上了。"

"他们谋杀了我们的六个小伙子。"

"谋杀可不好,吉姆。"

"绝对的。我太同意了。"

在接下来那令人不安的片刻间,他们的共识似乎让这场谈话失去了目的。吉姆可以听到电话那头的背景中传来吼声与枪声,还有群马的嘶鸣声,接着场景突然转换,法国圆号和弦乐器奏出辽阔的交响乐,让人想起开阔的沙漠,满是仙人掌和西部的孤丘。他努力寻找着安全的闲聊话题。"梅尔怎么样啦——"

可总统打断了他。"那事情——你知道的,反制主义——最近怎么样啦?"

"反转主义吗?棒极了。我们差不多就要启动了。这边的人都可兴奋了。这是一个历史性的转折点。"

"折腾出点事情来挺好的。让欧盟的日子难过点。"

"总统先生,我就是想要和你讨论这个。"

"给你两分钟。"

于是首相套用检察总长的词汇将这件事情分解了一番,还增添了一些他自己的生动意象,用水管和气象来作类比。一道喷涌的逆流,一股新近释放的能量顺着管道一路向上,轰隆一声炸塌了旧思维,轰开了旧障碍,最终,在爆发点或出水口,贸易协议还有资金,还有电子美元会像美丽的喷泉一样高高地射入空中,像久旱逢甘霖一样洒向大地,像大风卷挟着秋叶,像漩涡风暴中的雪花一样倾盆而下……

"我的账户?"总统用粗哑的嗓音问道,"你是说打进我的账户?"

"离岸账户,当然了。你应该让你自己的人核实一下。"

一阵沉默,打破它的只有电视发出的那起伏的轻声:大笑声,下等酒吧的钢琴声,碰杯的叮当声,还有庆功的鸣枪声。

终于:"你要是这么说的话,我看这里头或许有些道理。肯定有。我想,同心协力,我们可以让反制主义成功,吉姆。不过现在,我得,嗯……"

"最后一件事,总统先生。我能问你一件私人的事情吗?"

"当然。只要那不是关于——"

"不,不。当然不是。这事儿是关于……之前的。"

"什么之前,吉姆?"

"六?"

"再说一遍。"

"好吧。你……你以前……"

"以前什么?"

"有,唔……"

"天啊!有话快说,吉姆!有什么?"

他说出了那句悄悄话。"六条腿?"

电话挂断了。

*

个人与国家情绪的那个可靠的晴雨表——天气——陷入了动荡。一连五天的破纪录热浪之后是连续两周、席卷全国的破纪录降雨。同那些小河支流一样,泰晤士河的水位也上涨了,议会广场在四英寸深的河水还有密密麻麻、满目狼藉的塑料与卡纸漂浮物下面苟延残喘。再棒的摄影师也没法儿把这景色拍得诗情画意。雨水一停,高温再次从亚速尔群岛席卷而来,第二波持续时间更长的热浪开始了。整整一周,就在洪水退去后,伦敦的河滨区整个儿都覆盖在一层厚厚的、黏糊糊的淤泥下面。湿度从来没有降到过百分之九十以下。淤泥一干，沙尘就起了。灼热的大风席卷而来，狂暴得异乎寻常，一刮就是好几天，掀起了难得一见的都市沙尘暴，黄里透棕的沙幕厚得让人连纪念柱上的纳尔逊都看不见了。经过分析，一些沙子被认定居然是从撒哈拉沙漠来的。一只足有四英寸长的黑蝎子在博罗市场上售卖的一批鲜海枣中现身。狂热的社交媒体认定了这些毒虫能随风迁徙，定是驾着西南风从北非飘然而至的，要让他们改变想法则是不可能的任务。泛滥成灾的蝎子不由得让人想起了《圣经》中的话语。无论真假，它们让选民中一个人数可观的少数派愈发寝食难安了，这些人深信灾难就在眼前，一群不计后果的鲁莽空想家组成的政府推动着它的到来。另一群人数可观的少数派——比前一派声势稍大——则相信一场伟大的冒险就在眼前。他们已经迫不及待要让冒险开始了。两派在议会中都有代表，但都没能进入政府。这天气很准确。动荡和低可见度席卷了一切。

讨厌的是，那些渔民是被法国人一个接一个装进棺材送回来的，全都验了尸，拖了一个多礼拜。他们是用飞机送到斯坦斯特德机场的——不是吉姆希望在公众视野中现身的那种机场。在政府的坚持下，死者没有被立即移交给家人。相反，他们在剑桥机场外头被冷藏了起来，等到最后一人也从法国送回来以后，一架皇家空军运输机将六个人全部空运到了皇家伍顿·巴塞特镇。吉姆亲自操刀策划。他决定不要军乐队。相反，他会孤身一人站在机场跑道上，默默地面对摄影师和那架庞大的四引擎螺旋桨飞机，直到它在眼前滑停。一个勇敢而孤独的身影，直面机器巨兽。吉姆的触角对于公众情绪非常敏感。碰巧，连日的暴雨就是在那一天开始下的。那六具棺材全都覆盖着米字旗，首尾相接，依次被抬下飞机，抬棺的是近卫步兵第一团，缓缓地迈着葬礼的方步，最后将棺材停放在首相的脚下。这雨下得好，他聪明地拒绝了伸来的雨伞，在倾盆大雨中立正。他脸上挂着的是泪水吗？这样想也有道理。全国都在这波来去匆匆的悲痛的怒涛中团结了起来。在赫尔港内和伦敦的皇家海军贝尔法斯特号边上,鲜花、泰迪熊和玩具渔船堆成了四十英尺高的小山。

接着,第二场热浪来了。缩在炙热的屋顶下面,窗户在飞沙走石的大风中紧闭,首相的套间暖和得异乎寻常。可吉姆在这样的湿热中精神抖擞。他感觉身体从来没有这么好过。他的血液在刺激和稀释的作用下飞快地涌遍全身,用全新的想法滋养他忙碌的头脑。他拒绝任命一个新的特别顾问来替代西蒙。内阁会议也被他一脚踢开了。"实现反转"是他唯一的目标,为此他全力以赴,一如他在议会上的承诺。反转主义占据了他,他已经不知为何,也不知如何了。他进入了一种近乎无意识的极乐状态,忘记了时间,忘记了饥饿,甚至忘记了他自己的身份。他已然走火入魔,胸中燃烧着奇怪的激情,充斥着滚烫的渴望,迫不及待地要求解释,要求细节,要求修正。他依稀想起了1940年的丘吉尔,受其鞭策,他在每一份书面指示的后面都添了一句附言:"今天就要向我汇报,确认上述事宜已完成。"这句话也让媒体得知了。首相还同军情五处和军情六处的首脑、商界与工会领袖、医生、护士、农民、校长、典狱长、大学常务副校长等各色人等开会。他不喜欢回答问题，而是耐心地向众人解释他们各自的领域将如何在新体制下蓬勃发展。他还定期与党鞭长进行磋商。看起来，反转主义会以二十票左右的优势轻易通过。首相还写备忘录，发布命令，给他的内阁团队打电话鼓劲，给雪莉发去鼓舞人心的新闻稿。行政部门现在真的进入了涡轮增压状态；全伦敦的各个政府大楼整夜整夜地灯火通明。而唐宁街的那个套间也是如此。屋外，不分昼夜，跨着摩托的通信员们排起长队等着收发文件——这些文件过于机要，不能轻易交给数码传输机。

放眼全局，事态的发展也很喜人。普罗旺斯一家英国人所有的农场被法国爱国者泼上了红油漆。伦敦的各家小报全都义愤填膺。在首相宣称法国总统拉鲁塞本人应当为此负责后，头长着吉姆的脸、手舞大棒的约翰牛形象出现在了《太阳报》的一幅卡通里，接着传遍了网络。在民调中，山姆斯领先了霍勒斯·克雷布十五个点。在他的清晨推文中，美国总统形容山姆斯首相是一个"了不起的人"，宣布是时候将整个美国经济反转过来了。吃午饭前，道琼斯已经跌去一千点了。第二天早上，特普又改主意了。他只是，用他的话说，"随便一想"。全球股市吃了颗定心丸。可当美联储主席不屑一顾地称反转主义是"发神经"时，总统又愤怒地走回了老路。反转主义又回来了。它会让"旧精英们跪地求饶"。这一回道琼斯指数波澜不惊。就像一位华尔街知情人说的那样，市场会等到该恐慌的时候再恐慌。

那天深夜，敲门进来向他通报消息的正是第一天早上过来叫醒吉姆的那个裤装姑娘格洛里亚。西蒙被人发现用一根拖索吊死在了伊尔福德镇的自家卧室里，生前他一个人在家中独居。更妙的是，他没有留字条。他已经死了至少有一周了。趁着格洛里亚下楼拿香槟的当儿，吉姆匆匆写了一页表达赞赏与遗憾的便笺。西蒙没有写回忆录，也没有和"方案"的敌人暗通款曲，真是好样的。格洛里亚道了晚安，将那份尚有余温的颂词——感人至深，所有人都会这么说的——拿下楼去，交给雪莉打印发稿。首相独饮了那瓶香槟，一边继续着工作。可他平日的专注力似乎涣散了一点点。不知是什么在让他心神不宁，一个他很难证明的疑虑就像一个吐着线头的小小线团。最后，他不得不放下笔，把这件事情想清楚。归根结底，这不过是一个微不足道的迷信，而他——一个最最理性的生物——也无法将其祛退：最近传来的全是好消息——振奋人心的工作进度，党鞭长的估算，1922委员会的叛乱被瓦解，那几个渔民的死，他的报刊舆论，他扶摇直上的支持率，那桶红油漆，特普的赞扬，现在又来了这么一出。他真的是在无事自扰吗？可他毕生的经验都在告诉他，好运连连，必不长久。智穷计尽的西蒙让首相心头犯紧。他夜不能寐，整晚都在担心这个快乐的死讯预示着一个转折点。

第二天早上，转折真的来了，而且不是一个，而是两个，全都指向同一个方向。第一个转折是以党鞭长清晨的一封邮件的形式现身的。他手下的后座议员当中有一个阴谋小集团，一群在伦敦城外某处私宅密会的顺时派。关于他们所知甚少，他们的人数和姓名无人知晓。某些人有明显的嫌疑，但没有证据，只有泰然自若的矢口否认。到目前为止，他们一直投票支持政府，以隐藏他们的真实身份。这真是一个谜团，或者说是一个奇迹：他们是怎么躲过党鞭办公室的监视的呢。不过有一件事情确定无疑。外交大臣本尼迪克特·圣约翰正是幕后推手，其动机很可能是在反转议案回到下院时，帮助反对派挫败议案。

首相洗漱更衣，走下楼梯的时候，这场丑陋的背叛一直压在他的心头。盛怒之下，他想打人，想砸东西。他的下级雇员们在走道里和他打招呼的时候，他费了些力气才挤出一张笑脸来。他太心无旁骛了，太大意了。他几天前就应该对付本尼迪克特·圣约翰了。他要是有行动自由的话，一定很乐意一斧头砍断那人的喉咙。直到他坐下来享用咖啡，他那位双唇紧闭的新闻秘书把《每日电讯报》的一篇横跨两个版面的长文在他面前摊开时,这些狂怒、暴力的想法才开始从他的脑中淡去。

摆在他面前的是从政府内层核心拿到的泄密爆料——这家报纸最擅长干这个了,他们似乎根本不在乎这份爆料有悖于其严格的反转主义立场与原则。独家新闻的诱惑实在是难以抗拒。这是对皇家海军备忘录的一篇条理清晰的归纳,揭示了罗斯科夫事件其实是一场意外。文章很难质疑:雷达与卫星数据,监听到的渔船对海岸的通信、救生潜水员对军舰的通信、法国大使馆与爱丽舍宫的通信,还有目击证人的报告。吉姆把文章从头到尾读了两遍。里头的所有信息,西蒙都绝无可能染指。挤在一堆表格和照片当中的是一幅他自己的照片,一身雨水,肃立在机场上,身边是覆盖着国旗的六具棺椁。这份爆料是一场政治算计,显然是顺时派鼓动的一场袭击。消息来源显而易见。这两个坏消息是彼此关联的。他的敌人在出击,反转主义有危险。吉姆知道他必须迅速行动。

雪莉的办公室已经准备好了一份新闻稿。吉姆把稿子通读了一遍,删除了所有有向法国人道歉之嫌的暗示。这是一个不错的防守姿态。他不打算接受采访。总而言之,首相无比欣慰地得知拉金号船员的遭遇只是一场悲剧性事故的结果。摆在这里的——感谢我们勇敢的皇家海军——是无可辩驳的证据,而法国政府出于他们自己的某些理由,一直没能提供这些证据。遇难船员的家人所承受的可怕损失依然深深地……(等等)痛失亲人……(等等)。尽管法国当局有着种种……(等等等等),首相依然感谢他们,并希望向我们的好邻居保证,我们对于他们的无线电和电话通信的日常监听只不过是在诚挚地表达英国对于第五共和国的深深敬意以及……(等等,等等,等等)。

他认可了稿子,上楼回房的时候,顺道告诉手下不得打扰他。回到套间,他锁上门,清空咖啡桌上的文件,在桌子中央摆好一大本记事簿和一支红墨圆珠笔。他在桌前坐下,踌躇着,手托下巴,接着开始写下名字,在名字上画圈,用单线条或双线条把圆圈连接起来，再添上箭头和问号等修饰符。他在透过结盟、决裂和丑闻那扭曲失真的棱镜，评估各种行动及可能造成的后果，行动是否易暴露又是否易抵赖。他有一颗绝对精准又绝对冷静的头脑，在漫漫的时间长河中，通过遗传而完美适应了生存的艺术与种群的壮大。况且，他的一生都在进行永无止歇、有如家常便饭的斗争，他那项举重若轻的本领因而被淬炼得炉火纯青：他精通如何捍卫他所拥有的一切——同时却又不露声色。他镇定自若，因为他知道笑到最后的人一定是他。在这个酝酿计谋的时刻，他有着完全的自我意识，充分品味着最为纯粹的政治的乐趣——那便是为达目的不惜代价。他努力地思考着，算计着；半小时后，他认清了一件事：现在派人谋杀外交大臣为时已晚。他翻开新的一页白纸，盘忖着。

还有另一些更温柔的谋杀方式。当代的社会生活就像是一个军械库，塞满了最新设计的武器以及连着炸弹的绊线，淬毒的飞镖，还有地雷，就等有人一不小心踩将上去。这一回吉姆没有犹豫。他花了两个小时写了那篇文章，也许是投给《卫报》的。这篇像是某种自白的文字要求他具备一项他此前全然陌生的本领，那便是进入另一个人的头脑。他坚持了下来，三段之内，他已经开始感到难过了，为他自己，或者说是为那个他必须先找到，再诱骗的自我。或者是威胁。这是一个没有预定方向的开放式阴谋。你只有一边写，才能一边发现它。终于完事儿后，他按捺不住狂喜之情，在狭窄的阁楼空间里来回踱步。再没有什么比滴水不漏、环环相扣的一连串谎言更放飞自我的了。看来，这就是为什么有人会去当作家。接着他又坐回位子上，一只手悬停在电话跟前。他的清单上有三个名字。谁是他可以信赖的？或者说，谁是他最少怀疑的？他刚刚对自己问出这个问题，心中便立刻知道了答案，而他的食指已经开始拨号了。

*

关于简·菲什，有一件事情是人尽皆知的，那便是她抽烟斗。可同样人尽皆知的是，其实吧，她并不抽烟斗。她甚至都不抽烟。许多年前，她初出道时，担任的是政府里最卑微、最可怜、最不受欢迎的工作——北爱尔兰事务大臣。有一回，她在贝尔法斯特出席了反吸烟慈善组织举办的一场活动。她自愿吸了一口烟斗，然后把烟气喷到了一个孩子的脸上，以此凸显二手烟的危害。小女孩的眼睛闭着，也没有吸气。但公共生活需要大胆豪放的手笔。一如既往，一场持续两天的媒体风暴接踵而至。菲什坦率敢言，经常上新闻，还长了一张讨人喜欢、无甚特别的脸，漫画师们因此别无选择，只能让她叼住那只烟斗不放了。对于政治小品作家而言，她永远都将是"抽烟斗的简·菲什"。她很受欢迎。在可选政见的光谱中，她大体上属于务实派，因为其坚决反对当众哺乳的态度而甚受民众喜爱。她曾经是一个热诚的顺时派，直到她出于尊重人民的意愿，转而又成了一个热诚的反转派。她为这前后两个立场所作的精彩辩护都赢得了人们的赞赏。

他清单上的这三个女人当中,她是——在首相看来——最为接近她的信息素之源的。他的判断很准。当晚通电话的时候,在他罗列了各种事实后,她立刻就明白了采取坚决行动的必要性。她坦白说,她一直对本尼迪克特有疑虑。吉姆立马派人骑着摩托将他那份用封口文件袋装好的手稿送到了她手中。九十分钟后,她回电告知了几处她建议的改动。一些涉及历史细节问题;另一些,用她的话讲,是"说话的声音像不像的问题"。第二天一早,雪莉将那份乱糟糟的手稿打印出来,去了国王十字,把稿子投到了《卫报》主编的手中,并和主编商谈了一番。首相坚持要新闻秘书在文章付梓的时候驻守报社。这是一份思想开放的报纸,曾经在言论版上登过奥斯马·本·拉登的专栏,还雇用了极端组织"伊斯兰解放党"的一名铁杆成员当记者。要让他们登一篇简·菲什的文章是有点难,可是此刻,就在他们所鄙视的这届政府内,一个大臣正要对另一个大臣下死手,一家顺时派报纸怎能抵抗得了这样的诱惑?

当一家大报社只有几个钟头的时间来厘清一个重大素材时,其场面真是既让人惊叹,又激动人心。深厚的专业素养与团队合作,过目不忘的本领与快速分析的能力……各般武艺尽显神通。整栋大楼都在忙碌着。雪莉事后告诉手下,那景象就像是一场血战达到最高潮之时的战地医院。整个头版都天翻地覆了,连同里面的三个版面,还有主编的一篇亲笔社论。到了当天下午五点,第一批报纸已经从印刷机中问世了。对于老派的报人而言,当他们手捧一份新鲜出炉的实体报纸的时候,那也许是一个巅峰时刻。可这无关紧要。在此之前,报纸的网页已经进行了整整四个小时的事件揭秘了,并且不断地做着内容更新。其他的报社有足够的时间准备好用明天的版面接力报道这件大事,晚间电视新闻也有足够的时间调整他们的节目顺序。社交媒体、博客、政治网络杂志也全被点着了。罗斯科夫事件连同其琐碎的历史细节(说好的谋杀原来仅仅是意外)全都被挤下了榜单。如果说首相是错怪了法国人,那他也只是和大家一样弄错了而已。见不得人的勾当不在布列塔尼近海，却在白厅内部。一个担任国家顶级要职的官员身败名裂。外交大臣在哪里？他打算什么时候辞职？政府要怎么处理这场危机？这对反转主义意味着什么？有权有势的男人们什么时候会改过自新？对于最后一个问题，首相的回答只有两个字。

四

全文长两千八百五十七字，用一种与其说是报复，不如说是痛惜的语调写就。这个故事讲的是骚扰、霸凌、下流挑逗与不当触摸，它们轮番上演，最后全都通向言语暴力。菲什特地强调，强奸行为并没有实际发生，这为她的故事平添了几分可信度。这个大大咧咧、心直口快的北方女人竟然用如此袒露内心的细腻敏感讲述这些事情，这让很多人流下了眼泪。就连一个副主编的眼眶也湿了。这些可怕的事情发生在十五年前，持续了二十个月，那时简·菲什是本尼迪克特·圣约翰的议会私人秘书，而圣约翰则是就业与退休保障大臣。从那以后她一直遭受着内心折磨，出于对自己职业生涯的担心，出于屈辱，她不敢将事情说出来，同时又对她这位颇有才干的同事心生一种奇怪的保护欲。直到现在她才打破了沉默，因为外交大臣最小的孩子年满十八周岁了，而且她终于认识到,她有责任保护那些年轻一代的女性,她们也像曾经的她那样,工作在一些易受伤害的岗位上。头版的大字标题是:"外交大臣之耻"。一张当年的照片展示着菲什拿着圣约翰的行李,跟随他登上列车的画面。围绕着文章主体板块的是一些解释性与分析性的文本框。主编在她的社论中痛斥如此恶劣的行为,但同时告诫人们不要过早下定论。在言论版中,一位比较年轻的《卫报》员工则直接裁定:受害者不仅永远正确,而且有权要求人们相信她。

那天下午,独自一人坐在内阁室里,读着手中的那份报纸,首相发现,自己总的说来更支持后者。他越是反复品读他亲手挥就的这篇文章,一面赞叹版面设计,就越是发现文章的可信。他不得不佩服简的厉害。如此恶毒、冷酷、没心没肺地撒谎。如此侮辱那些男权的真正受害者。他不由得想,不知他自己有没有这个胆量在这篇文章下面署上他的名字。在这几个版面的边框和界线之内,这篇报道产生了它自己的事实,在他的想象中那就像是一座核反应堆产生了它自己的热能一样。无论这些事情有没有发生过,它们完全有可能发生,它们可以轻易发生,它们一定发生了。它们发生了!他开始替简感到义愤填膺了。外交大臣是个混账。比那更糟的是,他还迟到了。

五分钟后,当圣约翰被人带进来的时候,吉姆还在读着报纸,这会儿当然是故意读给人看的,手里握着钢笔。两人没有打招呼,首相也没有站起来。他只是指了指对面的一把椅子。终于,他把报纸折起来收好,叹了口气,哀伤地摇了摇头。"哎……本尼迪克特呀。"

外交大臣没有回应。他继续用沉稳的目光瞪着吉姆。这很让人不安。为了打破沉默,首相又添了一句:"当然,这篇东西我一个字都不信。"

"不过?"圣约翰提示道,"你马上就该说'不过'了。"

"一点不错。不过,不过,不过。这对我们很不利。你知道这一点。在事情澄清之前,我需要你走人。"

"那是当然。"

又是一阵沉默。吉姆和善地说:"我知道以前这种事情是个什么情况。也就是躲在文件柜后面胡说八道两句。现在可不一样了。又是'Me Too',又是这个那个的。你的'不过'给你了。你必须走人。没得商量。我需要你的辞职信。"

本尼迪克特从桌子对面伸过手来,将报纸一把拽走,摊开在桌面上。"是你在背后搞的鬼。"

首相耸耸肩。"是你先向《电讯报》泄的密。"

"我们的消息全是真的。可你们的!"

"我们的现在也成真了,本尼迪克特。"吉姆瞟了一眼手表。"我说,非得要我动手开了你吗?"

外交大臣掏出一页一折四的纸来,甩在桌子上。

吉姆把纸摊开。标准套话。非常荣幸能够担任……无端的指控……干扰政府的宝贵工作。

"很好。行了。多花点时间陪陪你的密谋团伙吧。"

本尼迪克特·圣约翰眼睛都没眨一下。"我们会搞死你的,吉姆。"

在这样的交锋中,即便你没能说出收官之语,也一定得画出收官之笔。首相站起来的时候,按下了桌子下面的一个按钮。一切都精心安排过。一个大胡子警察走了进来,背着一把自动步枪。

"把他从正门带出去。走慢点,"吉姆说,"在他跨出大门前,别松开他的胳膊肘。"

两人握了手。"他们在外头等你呢,本尼。拍照时间。你要不要借把梳子?"

*

在收录欧盟法规与关税同盟贸易协定的那部近乎无穷无尽的全书中,没有一个条文阻止成员国反转其金融流向。那并不等同于许可——真的吗?开放社会的一条根本原则就是,法无禁止皆可为。在欧洲的东部边境之外,在极权国家里,国家不恩准,万事皆非法。在欧盟的大楼走廊里,没有人想过要把逆转货币流向列为不可接受的做法,因为没有人听说过这个念头。就算有人听说过，也很难明确依据哪条法律或哲学原则来判定其非法。向科学基本原理求助也于事无补。大家都知道，在所有的物理定律中，我们都找不到逻辑上的理由来规定某种给定的现象只能正向进行，不能反向倒退，除了一个例外。而那个著名的例外就是热力学第二定律。根据这个美妙的理念，时间必然只能朝一个方向流动。那么反转主义就是第二定律的一个特例，因此违背了定律！真的吗？这个问题在斯特拉斯堡议会里引发了激烈的辩论，一直持续到了议员们不得不移师布鲁塞尔的那天早上——布鲁塞尔是他们时时得去的。等到他们落地布鲁塞尔，打开行囊，用了一顿尚可的午餐之后，所有人都已经没了头绪，尽管有一位理论物理学家从欧洲原子核研究会专程赶来，在不到三个小时的时间里用一些有趣的公式把一切都解释得一清二楚。况且，第二天又有了一个新的问题。那位科学家所说的一切要是反转过来，是不是也一样正确？

这个问题，就像许多其他的问题一样，被搁置在了一旁。一场有关摩尔多瓦冰淇淋的激烈争论迫在眉睫。这个议题并非像仇欧的伦敦媒体所佯称的那般无聊。让这种高品质的摩尔多瓦产品的成分符合欧盟标准的努力正是西方与俄国为了这个战略位置重要的小国的未来而日趋紧张的外交关系的一个缩影。这是一件复杂的事务，但至少在理论上，它是有解的。反转主义就完全不一样了。

当全民公投做出了那个令人震惊的决定时，布鲁塞尔的普通官员们诧异地在一旁看着。接着，不出所料，当整个流程陷入了错综复杂的泥沼中止步不前时，人们到底还是松了口气，耸了耸肩。毫无疑问，这通胡闹将以历史悠久的传统方式被束之高阁。可近日来，一件更令人们诧异的事情是，前怕狼后怕虎的好好先生山姆斯好像性情大变，改头换面，成了一位当代的伯里克利，凭着巧妙的手腕与狂暴的激情，誓把反转主义推行到底，不成功便成仁，无论欧训支不支持。这件事真的要实现了吗？难道议会母亲不能让这个国家恢复理智吗?难道一个想找乐子的布鲁塞尔伙计真能在伦敦豪华酒店里度过一个奢靡的周末,然后手握三千英镑离开收银台?还是说他当天就会因非法占有现金而被捕?还是说,他至少会在离境的时候被收缴现金?还是说——多么可怕啊——他会被迫在酒店厨房里买一份洗盘子的工作,直到现金花光?一个国家怎么能对自己做这样的事情?真可悲。真可笑。希腊人肯定有一个词来形容这件事吧?——选择一种对自己最不利的行为方式。没错,他们有。那就是 *akrasia*①。完美。这个词开始流传了。

然而,当美国总统的推特开始在这个话题上表现出某种程度的执着时,那些困惑、厌倦或屈尊俯就的笑容开始凝固了。以自由贸易、美国繁荣与伟大的名义,以造福穷人的名义,反转主义很"好"。山姆斯首相很"伟大"。另外,特普总统还提议让一位当过将军、现在开连锁赌场的亿万富翁

---

① 源于希腊语,本意为"无自我节制,不能自控",更主要是指在作出理性判断之后,因情势驱使而做出违背理性行为的这种品质。

老板来当英国国民保健制度的新"沙皇"。这让布鲁塞尔的有些人很不舒服,尽管依照欧盟的权力自主原则,这纯属内政。出于种种这些理由,首相于十二月初在北约总部发表演讲的时候,听众们给与了他非同寻常的礼遇。

山姆斯是代替他那位名誉扫地的外交大臣前往北约总部的。他的讲话并没有透露出任何新的实质性内容,除了一点:紧迫感。首相开门见山。所有人都知道,英国将要在本月25日实现金融反转,同时也将时来运转。"记住这个日子!"他快活地高呼道。大家礼貌地微笑着。接着首相罗列了一系列的要求,这些对于演讲大厅里坐在听众中间的那些谈判人员来说早已是耳熟能详。欧盟要向英国支付来年一百一十五亿英镑的年费,第一笔付款将在1月1日到期。北约的第一笔付款还要等到六月份。欧盟对英国出口的所有商品都应附上现金,金额必须算上百分之二的通胀率。为了体现善意——说到这里,吉姆伸开双手,似乎要拥抱台下的所有人——英国向欧盟出口的所有商品,其随附金额也会算上同样的通胀率。关于美国的"运行方向",他也给出了保证和更进一步的技术性细节。在结语中,吉姆表达了他的愿景,希望很快"你们就能拨云见日"——这个表达让坐在大厅后面小格子间里的保加利亚翻译一头雾水。待到拨云见日时,首相说道,所有人都会"闭着眼睛跟随我们走向未来"。

演讲结束后,一位年轻的法国外交官在和一位同事同去赴宴的时候,被人听到说了这样一句话:"我不明白他们干吗要起立鼓掌。还鼓得这么响亮,这么持久。"

"因为,"他那位年长的同伴解释道,"他们厌恶他所说的一切。"

英国媒体将吉姆的演讲说成是一场胜利,这么讲也不无道理。

第二天,在柏林出现了尴尬的一刻。他去那里是和德国总理举行私人会晤的。这天她在国会大厦里事务繁忙。再三道歉后,她在私人办公室旁边的一间小会客室里见了他。除了两个翻译、两个书记、三个保镖、德国外交部长、英国大使与二等秘书之外,屋里也就没有旁人了。宾主入座后,一张古朴的橡木桌将两位领导人分隔开来。其他人就都只能站着了。首相的目光越过总理的肩膀,望向施普雷河对岸的一座博物馆。透过博物馆的平板玻璃窗,他能看见里面在举办一场有关柏林墙的历史展览。吉姆认识两个德语词:Auf(在)和Wiedersehen(团聚)。会晤进行到一半的时候,他开始玩儿真的了。他要求提高德国对英国出口汽车的随附金额;作为交换,英国也将提高对德国出口的格拉斯哥雷司令(其品质,他解释道,远超莱茵雷司令)的随附金额。

就在这时,总理打断了他。她用手肘撑住桌子,一只手按住额头,闭上了疲惫的眼睛。"*Warum*?"她说道,紧随着这个词的是一小团别的字词。接着又是,"*Warum ...*"这次是一大团字词。接着又是如此。最后,她紧闭着双眼,脑袋微微垂向桌面,说出了一个简单、悲切的·"*Warum*?"

翻译用不带感情的声音说道:"你为什么要这么做?为什么,出于何种目的,你要撕裂你的国家?为什么你要向你最好的朋友们强加这种要求,假装我们是你的敌人?为什么?"

吉姆的大脑一片空白。是的,在外奔波了这么久,他累了。房间里鸦雀无声。河对岸,一队小学生正在一个老师的身后列队,准备进入博物馆。站在他椅子正后方的英国女大使轻轻地清了清嗓子。屋子里很闷。怎么没有人开窗呢。首相的脑中飘过了许多有说服力的回答,虽然他并没有将它们说出口。因为那就是我们正在做的。因为那就是我们所相信的。因为那就是我们说过我们要做的。因为那就是人民说过他们想要的。因为我来力挽狂澜了。因为。说一千道一万,那就是唯一的回答:因为。

这时,理智开始回归,他如释重负地回想起了他前一天晚上演讲时说过的一个词。"再生,"他答道,"还有电动飞机。"在令人不安的片刻沉默之后,一切都汹涌而来了。谢天谢地。"因为,总理女士,我们想要变得清洁、绿色、繁荣、团结、自信且雄心万丈!"

当天下午,他坐进大使的豪华轿车,踏上了去往柏林国际机场的归途;就在他靠在轿车后座上打盹的时候,电话响了。

"坏消息,不好意思,"党鞭长说道,"我已经使出所有的威逼手段了。他们知道他们会被开除。可有十二三个人还是投奔本尼迪克特了。遭遇解职反倒提升了他的人气。他们也都不信菲什。或者说,他们反正都恨她。依照目前的形势,我们差了二十多票……吉姆,你在听吗?"

"我在听。"他终于说道。

"怎么办。"

"我在想。"

"议会休会,以图后举?"

"我在想。"

他透过防弹车窗,凝视着窗外。司机选择了一条迂回曲折的线路,沿着绿茵茵的窄道一路前行,车前车后都是随行的摩托警卫。他们一路驶过许多精心打理过的木屋,屋前都有四分之一英亩的花园，同样精心打理过。小别居，他心想。柏林有一种特别的灰色。一种平和而悦目的灰色。它在空气中，在淡沙黄色的土壤中，在斑驳的石墙中。甚至在草木中和郊区的花床中。那是一种维持思考所必需的清凉而开阔的灰色。吉姆沉思着，党鞭长等待着；这时，他感到心跳放缓了，他的思绪自动重组成了一个个匀整而独立的图案，就像他刚才路过的那些小房子。那就像是他拥有一个能够解决面前任何现代难题的远古大脑。就算没有信息素潜意识的深厚资源。或者是那无聊的互联网。没有纸笔。没有顾问。

他抬头望去。护送首相去往那架等待着他的皇家空军专机的汽车和摩托车队在重返主路前停下了。就在这时，一个问题在他的脑海中浮现了，就像是从一百英尺深的一口井底漂上来的。它袅袅现身的姿态是那么轻盈，那么美妙。摆出这个问题也是那么的轻而易举：全世界他最爱的人是谁？他立刻就知道了答案，他也清楚地知道了他要怎么做。

当阿尔奇·特普请一位生意伙伴安排一场临时会议，召集共和党的一众立法者以及他们所属的各家学会与智库时，没有人觉得奇怪。这种会很常见，会议预算充裕，大家敬神爱国，宾主同乐。会议的宗旨是反堕胎，支持宪法第二修正案，特别强调自由贸易。矿业、建筑、石油、国防、烟草与制药业的代表云集。吉姆现在想起来了，他自己也参加过几次这样的会议，在他成为党魁之前。他的脑海里全是美好的回忆：那些亲切富态、上了一定年纪的人物，那一张张喷了香水、胡茬剃得短短的粉脸，那些穿起小礼服来如鱼得水的先生们。（很少有女人参会，也没有有色人种。）一个和善的伙计慷慨地硬塞给他一份请帖，邀他去爱达荷州的一家百万英亩的大牧场做客。五分钟后，又有一位向他保证，路易斯安那的一座建于南北战争前的豪宅敞开大门欢迎他。这些人慷慨而友善，但对于任何气候变化的说法还有联合国、北约、欧盟等国际组织，他们往往充满敌意。不可避免的，他们对英国的反转方案产生了浓厚的兴趣，并为之慷慨解囊，尽管许多人认为反转主义更适合那些小国，而非美国。但或许特普能让他们回心转意。在过去的几年间，具有正确信仰的英国议员也时常受邀参会。不过这场匆匆安排的会议将以反转金融流向为主题。总统会作简短的主题发言。在众多国际来宾中间，有四十位亲政府的保守党议员。会场定在了华盛顿的一家酒店，酒店的所有人刚好就是阿尔奇·特普，这一巧合应该会给后面的议程增添一抹都是自己人的氛围。

对于英国代表团而言，会议的时间可谓不太凑巧。议会的日程表排得满满当当。唯一的对话是关于反转主义。大家对于背后捅刀的前外交大臣主导的那场叛乱多有担心。投票日定在了12月19日。这段时间的选区事务总是加倍地繁忙，还有家庭聚会与司空见惯的圣诞订婚。可这是一趟奢华的旅行：头等舱，六千平方英尺的超大套房，令人咋舌的五位数单日花销，与总统握手，还有总的说来兴奋激动的心情：美方对于英国方案的兴趣正与日俱增。更何况，首相给他们所有人都写了亲笔信，敦促他们出席会议。他自己不打算去。但他会派兰开斯特公爵领地大臣特雷弗·哥特代他出席。这位特雷弗·哥特是个呆瓜，时而冲动，常被人说成是个"二维平面人"。真没法子啊——议员们向同事、选区官员和家人道了歉，开始着手安排各自的"配对"。这是一种议会的惯例：当一位议员无法现身下院参加投票时，可以同对立党派的一位议员配对。两人会同时缺席，这样投票结果便不受影响。这种办法对支持政府的议员们格外有用，因为他们经常要因公出差。那些生了病、发了疯或是要参加葬礼的议员当然也用得上。

会议取得了巨大的成功，一如既往。一开场，特普总统就说英国首相了不起，反转主义非常好。台下的众议员和参议员、寡头大亨与智库公知全都欢欣鼓舞：世界的走向正越来越接近他们的梦想。历史站在他们这边。12月18日的晚宴如同之前的几场宴席一样盛大。致辞结束后，在一整支交响乐队的伴奏下，一个模仿弗兰克·辛纳屈的演员用高亢的声线演绎了《我的路》。接着，一个神似葛罗莉亚·盖罗的歌手用一曲《我不会死》让七百名泪眼婆娑的宾客起立致敬。

就在大家重新落座的时候，那四十位英国客人的手机同时响了。党鞭长命令他们紧急返回伦敦。他们的车已经停在酒店门外了。他们的飞机两个钟头内起飞。他们有十分钟时间打点行装。他们要在第二天早上十一点钟前赶到下院，参加至关重要的反转法案投票。他们的配对约定被打破了。

英国人匆匆离开宴会厅，甚至都没时间和他们的新朋友道一声别。赶往罗纳德·里根机场的一路上，他们对工党同僚的咒骂声不绝于耳。真真是岂有此理：从乐园里被人生生给拖了出来，就因为他们愚蠢地信任了那些背信弃义的家伙。胸中的怒火让这群议员多半睡不着觉，于是他们变本加厉地痛饮酒水，一路骂到了希思罗机场。由于奇西克周边的交通拥堵，他们直到表决钟敲响前的几分钟才赶到下院。

直到这群"华盛顿狂欢客"——这就是他们已然摘得的名号——鱼贯走入大厅的时候,他们才注意到自己的配对伙伴并不在场。法案以27票的多数获得通过。剩下的,正如大家一上午反复在说的那样,就是"历史"了。第二天,反转法案获得御准,正式成为法律。

这,当然咯,是一场宪法丑闻,一桩耻辱。顺时派媒体发出愤怒的咆哮。四十位参与配对的工党议员联名在寄给《观察者报》的一封公开信上签字,谴责山姆斯政府"肮脏、无耻的手段"。还有人呼吁进行司法复审。

"我们经受得住这点风雨。不会有事的。你等着瞧吧。"山姆斯在电话中告诉简·菲什。随后,他又派人送了一箱香槟到党鞭长办公室。

那天晚上,他在BBC电视上做了一期长篇大论的访谈。他用严肃、理性的语调说道:"道歉?让我来阐释一些基本事实。我们这个国家并没有一部成文宪法。我们有的是传统和惯例。而这些都是我向来尊重的,哪怕这样做对我不利。现在，我要向你指出，打破配对协议是下院的一个光荣悠久的传统。就在不久前，不过是在我当上首相前，一位自由民主党女议员正在生产，而她的配对伙伴却在其党鞭的指示下，前往下院就一项正反双方势均力敌的议题投了票。众所周知，早在1976年，德高望重的迈克尔·海瑟尔丁就在下院中抓起议长权杖在空中挥舞，庆祝——你或许可以说——一场配对的破裂。二十年后，我们的三位议员不但和三位缺席的工党议员配了对，还和三位自民党议员配了对。工党无数次地打破配对协议。他们非常乐意在深夜的陌生人酒吧①里跟你讲这些故事。所有这些先例都牢牢确立了一个业已蔚然成风的欺诈传统。这样做在宪法上是正确的。它向世界表明了议会，归根结底，是一个是人就会犯错的好地方，正是这份人情味使它温馨而又充满活力。我还想补充一点：配对在重大议题投票中很不常见。当一件举足轻重的国家大事悬而

---

① 陌生人酒吧（Strangers' Bar），英国议会大厦里的一家酒吧，只对议员以及议会相关人员开放。

未决之时，把那些议员从华盛顿召回下院再正确不过了。当然，反对党在高呼这不公平。那是他们的工作。他们中还有些人对于霍勒斯·克雷布投票支持了我们很是生气。所以，我来回答你的问题：不道歉，绝对不道歉；无论是我还是我的任何一位政府成员都无须为任何事情道歉。"

今年没有白色圣诞节，不过也相去不远了。1月1日下了一场小雪，就在反转日公共假期前一天。两英寸的降雪没有吓住任何人。数以百万计的人流涌进商店，储备现金，好在假期结束后为返工买单。新政实行初期遇到了一些预料之中的困难。贾斯丁·比伯的演唱会上来了许多粉丝，个个都指望能领到钱。活动最后被取消了。还有人站在自动取款机前面，不知道该不该往以前塞银行卡的槽里面塞现金。可今年的一月销售额破了历史纪录。商店的货架被扫荡得干干净净——极大地提振了经济，一些人认为。圣基茨和尼维斯即将退出贸易协议的新闻几乎无人关注。

首相依然沉浸在圣诞节的气氛中，潇洒不羁地戴着一顶粉色的纸王冠，脱了鞋，摊手摊脚地躺在扶手椅上，手里端着一杯纯威士忌，在几位下属的陪同下，看着直升机航拍下的牛津大街上排了几英里的长队。有一句话他很想大声说出口，但最终还是选择将那几个字在脑海中默念了一遍：都结束了；他的任务完成了。很快他就会召集他的诸位同僚，通知他们：是时候开启重返大厦的远征，接受他们的部落对于英雄的欢呼了。

*

就在最后一场内阁会议召开前的那个午后，首相把所有的手下都打发回家，安排在正门外站岗的那个警察把门打开。所有的内阁成员都会把他们寄居的躯壳规规矩矩地停放在各自的部委办公桌前，等待着它们合法主人的归来。吉姆把自己的那具躯壳留在了顶楼的那张床上。对于这场会议，他制定了一项严格的着装标准：外骨骼。他本想着在内阁室的桌子上开会的，这样最合适，可等到他们在房间里碰头后，却发现上桌的路既长且险，因为桌子腿非常之光滑。所以，他们就改在屋子一角的一只废纸篓后面聚会，站成一个骄傲的圆圈。首相正要发表开场白，却被歌声给打断了——众蝇用中气十足但不太和谐的唧唧声，唱出了一曲《生日快乐》。唱罢他们赶忙紧张地望向门口。当班的警察没有听到他们。

内阁会议是以信息素进行的，其速度十倍于标准的英语语速。不等吉姆开口，简·菲什抢先发表了一通致谢词。她赞扬首相将"矢志不渝的精神同脱缰野马般的魅力与幽默罕有地结合在了一起"。英国现在独行于世间了。人民发话了。我党领袖的天才让他们跨过了那道线。他们的命运掌握在了他们自己的手中。反转主义实现了！不再有犹豫，不再有拖延！英国独行于世间了！

喊出那几句深入人心的口号后，她一时动情得无法自已，竟然哽咽了，可这没有关系。迎接她的发言的是热烈的起立鼓掌——甲壳和退化的翅翼摩擦出一片真诚的沙沙声。

接着，每一位内阁成员也都说上了几句，最后发言的是新任外交大臣汉弗莱·巴顿，刚刚从国防大臣的位置被提拔上来的。他领着众蠊又唱了一轮《因他是个大好人》。

发表演说前，首相先跨进了圆圈的中心。他一边讲话，一边激情澎湃地颤动着触须，身体缓缓地在原地旋转，吸引每位阁员的注意力。

"我亲爱的同僚们，感谢你们这些善意的想法。我深受触动。在我们的使命即将结束的这最后时刻，我们有责任守护真理。有一条真理是我们从未向我们卓越的国民隐瞒过的。要想让我们的工业、金融与贸易的强大引擎倒转，它们首先必须减速再停机。磨难是少不了的。甚至会有极端的艰难险阻。我毫不怀疑承受这一切将会磨砺这个伟大国度的人民。可那些都不是我们要关心的了。既然我们已经抛弃了我们那讨厌的临时躯体，我们就可以放心大胆地颂扬另一些更深层次的真理了。

"我们的种群至少有三亿年的悠久历史。就在四十年前，在这座城市里，我们还是一个被边缘化的群体，遭人鄙视，是人类挖苦和嘲弄的对象。往好里说，被忽视。往坏里说，被憎恶。可我们坚守住了我们的原则，我们的理念开始生根，开始进展缓慢，但随后越来越势不可挡。我们的核心信仰不可动摇：我们的行动永远是为了自利。正如我们的拉丁语名称*blattodea*暗示的那样，我们是避光的生物。我们理解黑暗，热爱黑暗。在最近的世代——这过去的两千年里，我们同人类比邻而居，也了解了他们对于黑暗的独特爱好，而在这一点上他们不像我们那么全心全意。可每当这种爱好在他们中间占了上风时，我们会欣欣向荣。凡是他们拥抱贫穷、肮脏、污秽的地方，我们就会发展壮大。通过迂回曲折的手段，经历了许许多多的实验与失败，我们终于弄清了导致人类衰颓的前提条件。战争与全球变暖是跑不掉的，还有——在和平时期——阶级固化，财富集中，根深蒂固的迷信，谣言，分裂，怀疑科学、智识、陌生人与社会合作。你们了解这份清单。在过去，我们经受了巨大的困难，包括下水道的修建、人类对净水的可恶嗜好、对疾病的病菌学阐释、国与国间的和平协定。我们的数量确实因为这些以及许多别的打击而锐减。但我们反击了。而现在,我希望并且相信我们已经创造了实现复兴的必要条件。当那种奇怪的疯病——反转主义——让人类大众走向贫困时——这一点必将实现——我们定会兴旺发达。如果说善良体面的普通人被蒙蔽了,要受苦了,那么,他们一定会非常欣慰地得知,别的善良体面的种群——比如说我们自己——将会收获更多的幸福,与此同时我们的数量将与日俱增。全世界的福祉净值并没有减少。公平依然是一个常量。

"过去的几个月里,为了我们的使命你们殚精竭虑。我祝贺你们,感谢你们。正如你们发现的那样,做一个'现代智人'不是一件容易的事。他们的欲望时常与他们的智商冲突角力。不像我们——我们是完整统一的。你们每个人都找到了一副人类的肩膀去拉动民粹主义的车轮。你们已经看到了你们劳动的果实,因为那车轮开始转了。现在,我的朋友们，是时候踏上我们南下的旅程了。回我们亲爱的家园吧！请大家排成一字纵队。出门的时候记得左转。"

有一件事他并没有提，但他知道他的每一位内阁成员都清楚前方的险阻。这是一个多云的午后，他们从敞开的大门溜出，经过那个当班警察的时候，刚刚过了下午四点。他们喜欢这冬日的阴郁。也正因为此，他们才没有看到一个小东西正急匆匆地奔向唐宁街10号，去再续它的人生。不到半个钟头，吉姆的队伍已经钻过唐宁街的大门，进入了白厅街。他们穿过人行道，爬进了下面的阴沟。那座马粪山早就不见了。晚高峰时间的那一片移动森林般的脚步从他们的头顶上方隆隆地踩过。他们花了九十分钟才抵达议会广场，就在这里，悲剧发生了。当时他们正等着红灯变绿灯，准备百米冲刺过马路。可兰开斯特公爵领地大臣特雷弗·哥特太性急了——他时常这样——抢跑了一步，结果消失在了一台垃圾车的车轮底下。车流一停，整个内阁班子赶忙跑上马路救他。他仰面躺着，真的被压成了二维平面。从他的甲壳下面汩汩渗出了一团黏稠的奶白色物质——那可是一道人见人爱的珍馐。今晚会有一场英雄的盛宴,他们又有那么多的奇闻逸事要讲述,何其乐哉!赶在绿灯又变回红灯前,他的同僚们争分夺秒地抬起他,将那团分泌物虔敬地放在他的下腹部上面。接着,六位阁员一人抓住一条腿,抬着他奔向了议会大厦。

The Cockroach

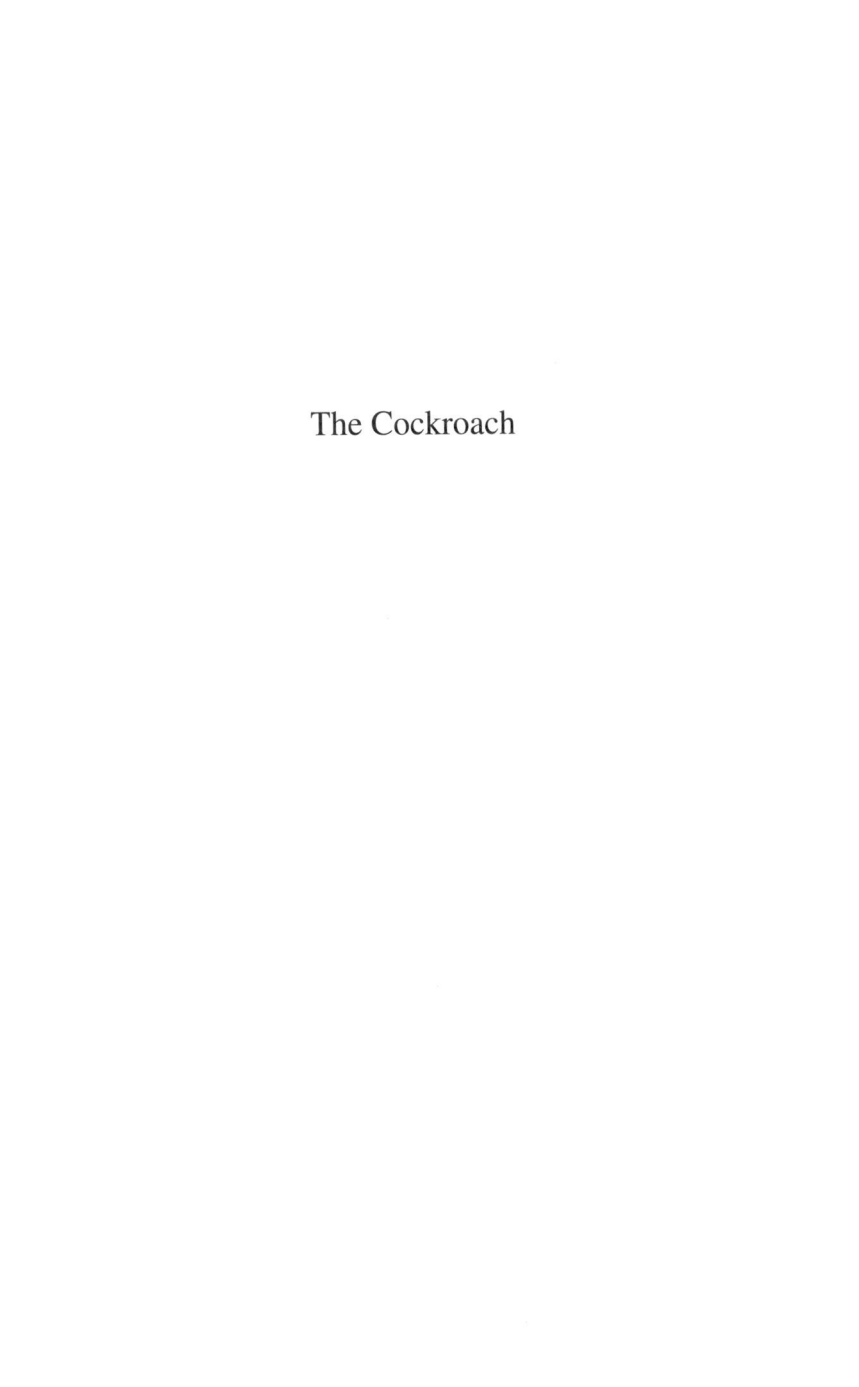

Preface

By way of dogged, exacting negotiation by one Prime Minister then another, parliamentary chaos and paralysis, two general elections, and bitter division across the country, Great Britain has lately been attempting to fulfil the most pointless, masochistic ambition ever dreamed of in the history of these islands. The rest of the world, Presidents Putin and Trump excepted, have watched on in dismay. If we ever manage to leave the European Union, we will then begin the hopeful fifteen-year trudge, back towards some semblance of where we once were, with our multiple trade deals, security and scientific co-operation and a thousand other useful arrangements. Why are we doing this to ourselves? My cockroach Prime Minister gives the German Chancellor the only possible answer: *because.*

The Cockroach was conceived at that point along this

journey when despair meets laughter. Many people have wondered whether the process of Brexit is beyond satire. What wicked novelist could have dreamed it up? It is in itself a tortuous self-satire. Perhaps all that's possible is mockery and the sad consolations of laughter.

Whether or not our Brexit moment finally arrives, we will be asking ourselves questions for a very long time. Lies, dodgy funding, Russian involvement will preoccupy future historians. And they will surely study the blindness caused by a special kind of magic dust common to all the populist movements currently gripping Europe, the USA, Brazil, India and many other countries. The ingredients of this dust are well-known by now: wild unreason, hostility to strangers, resistance to patient analysis, distrust of 'experts', a swaggering regard for one's own country, a passionate belief in simple solutions, a longing for cultural 'purity' -and a handful of cynical politicians to exploit these impulses.

Of course, local conditions vary. In Brazil they prefer

to burn down the Amazon rain forest. The USA longs for its Mexican Wall. Turkey has perfected the art of locking up journalists. In Britain, as the magic dust closed our eyes, we learned that the long-evolved ecology of the EU has profoundly shaped the flora of our nation's landscape. To rip out these plants is proving brutal and not, after all, very simple. But that has stopped no one. We will press on-*because*.

There is much that is historically unjust about the British state, but very little of that injustice derives from the EU. It was the task of the Brexiters to persuade the electorate otherwise. They succeeded with 37%, enough to transform our collective fate for many years to come. In classic populist magic dust style, Brexiter hedge fund owners, plutocrats, Etonians and newspaper proprietors cast themselves as enemies of the elite. It worked, and now that elite of anti clitists has become our government.

In the English literary tradition of political satire, the foundational text remains Jonathan Swift's *A Modest*

Proposal. I read it for the first time when I was sixteen. Its unblinking assertion that cooking then eating babies would be a solution to a long-standing problem was savage and grotesque, but only as cruel, in Swift's view, as English dominion in Ireland.

With Brexit, something ugly and alien entered the spirit of our politics and to me it seemed reasonable to conjure a cockroach, that most despised of living forms. Kafka's *Metamorphosis* lies in the path of any attempt to conjure a physical exchange between human and insect, but after the necessary bow of acknowledgement, it was to Swift that I turned. The task was always to devise a political and economic project that might equal the self-defeating absurdity of Brexit. I cannot be sure that I succeeded with my ludicrous concoction, Reversalism. Given the magnitude of the national project and its likely impact on us for at least a generation to come, perhaps nothing can match the scale of its folly.

Nearly two thirds of the British electorate did not

vote to leave the European Union. Most of business, agriculture, science, finance and the arts were against the Brexit project. Three quarters of MPs voted to remain in the EU, but most of them ignored public interest and shrank behind party loyalties and 'the people have spoken' – that bleak Soviet locution, that mind-clouding magic dust which has blinded reason and obscured our children's prospects to live and work freely in continental Europe.

Populism, oblivious to its own ignorance, with murmurs of blood and soil, impossible nativist yearnings and tragic contempt for climate change concerns, might in the future conjure other monsters, some of them far more violent, more consequential than Brexit. But in all versions, the spirit of the cockroach will thrive. We should get to know this creature well, the better to defeat it. I believe we will.

If reason doesn't open its eyes and prevail, then we may have to count on laughter.

To Timothy Garton Ash

This novella is a work of fiction. Names and characters are the product of the author's imagination and any resemblance to actual cockroaches, living or dead, is entirely coincidental.

ONE

That morning, Jim Sams, clever but by no means profound, woke from uneasy dreams to find himself transformed into a gigantic creature. For a good while he remained on his back (not his favourite posture) and regarded his distant feet, his paucity of limbs, with consternation. A mere four, of course, and quite unmoveable. His own little brown legs, for which he was already feeling some nostalgia, would have been waving merrily in the air, however hopelessly. He lay still, determined not to panic. An organ, a slab of slippery meat, lay squat and wet in his mouth – revolting, especially when it moved of its own accord to explore the vast cavern of his mouth and, he noted with muted alarm, slide across an immensity of teeth. He stared along the length of his body. His colouring, from shoulders to ankles, was a pale blue, with darker blue piping around his neck and wrists, and white buttons in a vertical line right down his unsegmented thorax. The light breeze that blew intermittently across it, bearing a not unattractive odour of decomposing food and grain alcohol, he accepted as his breath. His vision was unhelpfully narrowed – oh for a compound eye – and everything he saw was oppressively colourful. He was beginning to understand that by a grotesque reversal his vulnerable flesh now lay outside his skeleton, which was therefore wholly invisible to him. What a comfort it would have been to catch a glimpse of that homely nacreous brown.

All this was worrying enough, but as he came more fully awake he remembered that he was on an important, solitary mission, though for the moment he could not recall what it was. I'm going to be late, he thought, as he attempted to lift from the pillow a head that must have weighed as much as five kilos. This is so unfair, he told himself. I don't deserve this. His fragmentary dreams had been deep and wild, haunted by raucous, echoing voices in constant dissent. Only now, as this head slumped back, did he begin to see through to the far side of sleep and bring to mind a mosaic of memories, impressions and intentions that scattered as he tried to hold them down.

Yes, he had left the pleasantly decaying Palace of Westminster without even a farewell. That was how it had to be. Secrecy was all. He had known that without being told. But when exactly had he set out? Certainly it was after dark. Last night? The night before? He must have left by the underground car park. He would have passed the polished boots of the policeman at the entrance. Now he remembered. Keeping to the gutter, he had hurried along until he had reached the edge of the terrifying crossing in Parliament Square. In front of a line of idling vehicles impatient to pestle him into the tarmac, he made a dash for the gutter on the far side. After which, it seemed a week passed before he crossed another terrifying road to reach the correct side of Whitehall. Then what? He had sprinted, surely, for many yards and then stopped. Why? It was coming back to him now. Breathing heavily through every tube in his body, he had rested near a wholesome drain to snack on a discarded slice of pizza. He couldn't eat it all, but he did his best. By good luck it was a margherita. His second favourite. No olives. Not on that portion.

His unmanageable head, he discovered, could rotate through 180 degrees with little effort. He turned it now to one side. It was a small attic bedroom, unpleasantly lit by the morning sun, for the curtains had not been drawn. There was a telephone at his bedside, no, two telephones. His constricted gaze travelled across the carpet to settle on the skirting board and the narrow gap along its lower edge. I might have squeezed under there out of the morning light, he thought sadly. I could have been happy. Across the room there was a sofa and by it, on a low table, a cut-glass tumbler and an empty bottle of scotch. Laid out over an armchair was a suit and a laundered, folded shirt. On a larger table near the window were two box files, one sitting on top of the other, both coloured red.

He was getting the hang of moving his eyes, now that he understood the way they smoothly swivelled together without his help. Rather than letting his tongue hang out beyond his lips, where it dripped from time to time onto his chest, he found it was more comfortably housed within the oozing confines of his mouth. Horrible. But he was acquiring the knack of steering his new form. He was a quick learner. What troubled him was the need to set about his business. There were important decisions to be taken. Suddenly, a movement on the floor caught his attention. It was a little creature, in his own previous form, no doubt the displaced owner of the body he now inhabited. He watched with a degree of protective interest as the tiny thing struggled over the strands of pile carpet, towards the door. There it hesitated, its twin antennae waving uncertainly with all of a beginner's ineptitude. Finally, it gathered its courage and stumbled under the door to begin a difficult, perilous descent. It was a long way back to the palace, and there would be much danger along the way. But if it made it without being squashed underfoot, it would find, behind the palace panelling or below the floorboards, safety and solace among millions of its siblings. He wished it well. But now he must attend to his own concerns.

And yet Jim did not stir. Nothing made sense, all movement was pointless until he could piece together the journey, the events, that had led him to an unfamiliar bedroom. After that chance meal he had scuttled along, barely conscious of the bustle above him, minding his own business as he hugged the shadows of the gutter, though for how long and how far was beyond recall. What he knew for certain was that he reached at last an obstacle that towered over him, a small mountain of dung, still warm and faintly steaming. Any other time, he would have rejoiced. He regarded himself as something of a connoisseur. He knew how to live well. This particular consignment he could instantly place. Who could mistake that nutty aroma, with hints of petroleum, banana skin and saddle soap. The Horse Guards! But what a mistake, to have eaten between meals. The margherita had left him with no appetite for excrement, however fresh or distinguished, nor any inclination, given his gathering exhaustion, to clamber all the way over it. He crouched in the mountain's shadow, on the springy ground of its foothills, and considered his options. After a moment's reflection, it was clear what he must do. He set about scaling the vertical granite wall of the kerb in order to circumvent the heap and descend on its far side.

Reclining now in the attic bedroom, he decided that this was the point at which he had parted company with his own free will, or the illusion of it, and had come under the influence of a greater, guiding force. Mounting the pavement, as he did, he submitted to the collective spirit. He was a tiny element in a scheme of a magnitude that no single individual could comprehend.

He heaved himself onto the top of the kerb, noting that the droppings extended a third of the way across the pavement. Then, out of nowhere, there came down upon him a sudden storm, the thunder of ten thousand feet, and chants and bells, whistles and trumpets. Yet another rowdy demonstration. So late in the evening. Loutish people making trouble when they should have been at home. Nowadays, these protests were staged almost every week. Disrupting vital services, preventing ordinary decent types from going about their lawful business. He froze on the kerb, expecting to be squashed at any moment. The soles of shoes fifteen times his own length slammed the ground inches from where he cowered and made his antennae and the pavement tremble. How fortunate for him that at one point he chose to look up, entirely in the spirit of fatalism. He was prepared to die.

But that was when he saw an opportunity – a gap in the procession. The next wave of protesters was fifty yards away. He saw their banners streaming, their flags bearing down, yellow stars on a blue ground. Union Jacks too. He had never scuttled so fast in his life. Breathing hard through all the trachea on his body segments, he gained the other side by a heavy iron gate seconds before they were on him again with thunderclaps of hideous tramping, and now catcalls and savage drumbeats. Seized by mortal fear and indignation, an inconvenient mix, he darted off the pavement and, to save his life, squeezed under the gate into the sanctuary and relative tranquillity of a side street where he instantly recognised the heel of a standard issue policeman's boot. Reassuring, as ever.

Then what? He proceeded along the empty pavement, past a row of exclusive residences. Here he was surely fulfilling the plan. The collective pheromonal unconscious of his kind bestowed on him an instinctive understanding of his direction of travel. After half an hour of uneventful progress, he paused, as he was meant to do. On the far side of the street was a group of a hundred or so photographers and reporters. On his side, he was level with and close by a door, outside which stood yet another policeman. And just then, that door swung open and a woman in high heels stepped out, almost spearing him right through his ninth and tenth abdominal segments. The door remained open. Perhaps a visitor was arriving. In those few seconds Jim looked into a welcoming, softly lit hallway, with skirting boards somewhat scuffed – always a good sign. On a sudden impulse that he now knew was not his own, he ran in.

He was doing well, given his unusual circumstances, lying on this unfamiliar bed, to recall such details. It was good to know that his brain, his mind, was much as it had always been. He remained, after all, his essential self. It was the surprising presence of a cat that had caused him to run, not in the direction of the skirting boards, but towards the stairs. He climbed three and looked back. The cat, a brown and white tabby, had not seen him, but Jim considered it dangerous to descend. So began his long climb. On the first floor there were too many people walking along the landing, in and out of rooms. More prospect of being trodden to death. An hour later, when he reached the second floor, the carpets were being vigorously vacuumed. He knew of many souls who had been lost that way, sucked into dusty oblivion. No choice but to keep on climbing until— but now, suddenly, here in the attic, all his thoughts were obliterated by the harsh ringing of one of the bedside telephones. Even though he found that he could at last move one of his limbs, an arm, he did not stir. He couldn't trust his voice.

And even if he could, what would he say? I'm not who you think I am? After four rings the phone went silent.

He lay back and allowed his frantic heart to settle. He practised moving his legs. At last, they stirred. But barely an inch. He tried again with an arm, and raised it until it towered far above his head. So, back to the story. He had heaved himself up the last step to arrive breathless on the top landing. He squeezed under the nearest door into a small apartment. Usually, he would have made straight for the kitchen but instead he climbed a bedpost and, utterly depleted, crept under a pillow. He must have slept deeply for— but now, dammit, there came a tapping sound and before he could respond, the door to the bedroom was opening. A young woman in a beige trouser suit stood on the threshold and gave a brisk nod before entering.

'I tried phoning but I thought I'd better come up. Prime Minister, it's almost seven thirty.'

He could think of no response.

The woman, clearly an aide of some kind, came into the room and picked up the empty bottle. Her manner was rather too familiar.

'Quite an evening, I see.'

It would not have done to remain silent for long. From his bed he aimed for an inarticulate sound, somewhere between a groan and a croak. Not bad. Higher pitched than he would have wanted, with a hint of a chirrup, but plausible enough.

The aide was gesturing towards the larger table, at the red boxes. 'I don't suppose you had a chance to, uh ...'

He played it safe by making the same sound again, this time on a lower note.

'Perhaps after breakfast you could take a ... I should remind you. It's Wednesday. Cabinet at nine. Priorities for government and PMQs at noon.'

Prime Minister's Questions. How many of those he had crouched through, listening enthralled from behind the rotten wainscoting in the company of a few thousand select acquaintances? How familiar he was with the opposition leader's shouted questions, the brilliant non sequitur replies, the festive jeers and clever imitations of sheep. It would be a dream come true, to be *primo uomo* in the weekly operetta. But was he adequately prepared? No less than anyone else, surely. Not after a quick glance at the papers. Like many of his kind, he rather fancied himself at the despatch box. He would be fast on his feet, even though he only had two.

In the space where once he sported a fine mandible, the unwholesome slab of dense tissue stirred and his first human word rolled out.

'Righto.'

'I'll have your coffee ready downstairs.'

He had often sipped coffee in the dead of night on the tea room floor. It tended to keep him awake in the day, but he enjoyed the taste and preferred it milky, with four sugars. He assumed this was generally known by his staff.

As soon as the aide had left the room, he pushed away the covers and managed at last to swing his tuberous legs onto the carpet. He stood at last at a vertiginous height, swaying slightly, with his soft, pale hands pressed to his forehead, and groaning again. Minutes later, making his unsteady way towards the bathroom, those same hands began nimbly to remove his pyjamas. He stepped out of them to stand on pleasantly heated tiles. It rather amused him, passing water thunderously into a specially prepared ceramic bowl, and his spirits lifted. But when he turned to confront the mirror over the handbasin, they sank again. The bristling oval disk of a face, wobbling on a thick pink stalk of neck, repelled him. The pinprick eyes shocked him. The inflated rim of darker flesh that framed an array of off-white teeth disgusted him. But I'm here for a proud cause and I'll put up with anything, he reassured himself as he watched his hands turn the taps and reach for his shaving brush and soap.

Five minutes later he felt nauseated as he paused, still swaying, before the prospect of putting on the clothes laid out for him. His own sort took great pride in their beautiful, gleaming bodies and would never have thought to cover them up. White underpants, black socks, a blue and white striped shirt, dark suit, black shoes. He observed with detachment the automatic speed with which his hands tied his laces, and then, back at the bathroom mirror, his tie. As he combed his gingery brown hair, he noticed with sudden homesickness that it was the same colour as his good old shell. At least something has survived of my looks, was his melancholy thought as, finally, he stood at the top of the stairs.

He began a dizzying descent, trusting his legs to carry him down safely as he had his hands to shave and dress him. He kept a firm grip on the bannisters, smothering a groan at each step. As he crossed the landings, where there were hairpin turns, he clung on with both hands. He could have passed for a man with a hangover. But what had taken an hour to climb up took only seven minutes to climb down. Waiting for him in the hallway at the foot of the stairs was a group of very young men and women, each holding a folder. Respectfully they murmured, 'Good morning, Prime Minister,' in a soft, uneven chorus. None of them dared look at him directly while they waited for him to speak.

He cleared his throat and managed to say, 'Let's get on, shall we.' He was stuck for any further remark, but luckily a fellow, older than the rest and wearing a suit as expensive-looking as his own, pushed through and, seizing Jim by the elbow, propelled him along the corridor.

'A quick word.'

A door swung open and they went through. 'Your coffee's in here.'

They were in the Cabinet room. Halfway down the long table by the largest chair was a tray of coffee, which the prime minister approached with such avidity that over the last few steps he broke into a run. He hoped to arrive ahead of his companion and snatch a moment with the sugar bowl. But by the time he was lowering himself into the chair, with minimal decorum, his coffee was being poured. There was no sugar on the tray. Not even milk. But in the grey shadow cast by his saucer, visible only to him, was a dying bluebottle. Every few seconds its wings trembled. With some effort, Jim wrenched his gaze away while he listened. He was beginning to think he might sneeze.

'About the 1922 Committee. The usual bloody suspects.'

'Ah, yes.'

'Last night.'

'Of course.'

When the bluebottle's wings shook they made the softest rustle of acquiescence.

'I'm glad you weren't there.'

When a bluebottle has been dead for more than ten minutes it tastes impossibly bitter. Barely alive or just deceased, it has a cheese flavour. Stilton, mostly.

'Yes?'

'It's a mutiny. And all over the morning papers.'

There was nothing to be done. The prime minister had to sneeze. He had felt it building. Probably the lack of dust. He gripped the chair. For an explosive instant he thought he had passed out.

'Bless you. There was talk of a no-confidence vote.'

When he opened his unhelpfully lidded eyes, the fly had gone. Blown away. 'Fuck.'

'That's what I thought.'

'Where is it? I mean, where's the sense in—'

'The usual. You're a closet Clockwiser. Not with the Project. Not a true go-it-alone man. Getting nothing through parliament. Zero backbone. That sort of thing.'

Jim drew his cup and saucer towards him. No. He lifted the stainless steel pot. Not under there either.

'I'm as Reversalist as any of them.'

By his silence his special adviser, if that was what he was, appeared to disagree. Then he said, 'We need a plan. And quick.'

It was only now that the Welsh accent was evident. Wales? A small country far to the west, hilly, rain-sodden, treacherous. Jim was finding that he knew things, different things. He knew differently. His understanding, like his vision, was narrowed. He lacked the broad and instant union with the entirety of his kind, the boundless resource of the oceanic pheromonal. But he had finally remembered in full his designated mission.

'What do you suggest?'

There came a loud single rap, the door opened and a tall man with a generous jaw, bottle-black swept-back hair and pinstripe suit strode in.

'Jim, Simon. Mind if I join you? Bad news. Encryption just in from—'

Simon interrupted. 'Benedict, this is private. Kindly bugger off.'

Without a shift in expression, the foreign secretary turned and left the room, closing the door behind him with exaggerated care.

'What I resent,' Simon said, 'about these privately educated types is their sense of entitlement. Excluding you, of course.'

'Quite. What's the plan?'

'You've said it yourself. Take a step towards the hardliners, they scream for more. Give them what they want, they piss on you. Things go wrong with the Project, they blame anyone and everyone. Especially you.'

'So?'

'There's a wobble in the public mood. The focus groups are telling a new story. Our pollster phoned in the results last night. There's general weariness. Creeping fear of the unknown. Anxiety about what they voted for, what they've unleashed.'

'I heard about those results,' the prime minister lied. It was important to maintain face.

'Here's the point. We should isolate the hardliners. Confidence motion my arse! Prorogue parliament for a few months. Astound the bastards. Or even better, change tack. Swing—'

'Really?'

'I mean it. You've got to swing—'

'Clockwise?'

'Yes! Parliament will fall at your feet. You'll have a majority – just.'

'But the will of the p—'

'Fuck the lot of them. Gullible wankers. It's a parliamentary democracy and you're in charge. The house is stalled. The country's tearing itself apart. We had that ultra-Reversalist beheading a Clockwise MP in a supermarket. A Clockwise yob pouring milkshake over a high-profile Reversalist.'

'That was shocking,' the prime minister agreed. 'His blazer had only just been cleaned.'

'The whole thing's a mess. Jim, time to call it off.' Then he added softly, 'It's in your power.'

The PM stared into his adviser's face, taking it in for the first time. It was narrow and long, hollow at the temples, with little brown eyes and a tight rosebud mouth. He had a grey three-day beard and wore trainers and a black silk suit over a Superman T-shirt.

'What you're saying is very interesting,' the PM said at last.

'It's my job to keep you in office and this is the only way.'

'It'd be a ... a ...' Jim struggled for the word. He knew several variants in pheromone, but they were fading. Then he had it. 'A U-turn!'

'Not quite. I've been back through some of your speeches. Enough there to get you off the hook. Difficulties. Doubts. Delays. Sort of stuff the hardliners hate you for. Shirley can prepare the ground.'

'Very interesting indeed.' Jim stood up and stretched. 'I need to talk to Shirley myself before Cabinet. And I'll need a few minutes alone.'

He began to walk round the long table towards the door. He was coming to feel some pleasure in his stride and a new sense of control. Improbable as it had seemed, it was possible to feel stable on only two feet. It hardly bothered him to be so far off the ground. And he was glad now not to have eaten a bluebottle in another man's presence. It might not have gone down well.

Simon said, 'I'll wait for your thoughts, then.'

Jim reached the door and let the fingers of one strange hand rest lightly on the handle. Yes, he could drive this soft new machine. He turned, taking pleasure in doing it slowly, until he was facing the adviser, who had not moved from his chair.

'You can have them now. I want your resignation letter on my desk within the half hour and I want you out of the building by eleven.'

*

The press secretary, Shirley, a tiny, affable woman dressed entirely in black and wearing outsized black-rimmed glasses, bore an uncomfortable resemblance to a hostile stag beetle. But she and the PM got on well as she fanned out before him a slew of unfriendly headlines. 'Bin Dim Jim!' 'In the name of God, go!' Following Simon's usage and calling the hard-line Reversalists on the backbenches 'the usual bloody suspects' helped give the news a harmless and comic aspect. Together, Jim and Shirley chuckled. But the more serious papers agreed that a no-confidence vote might well succeed. The prime minister had alienated both the Clockwise and Reversalist tendencies within his party. He was too much the appeaser. By reaching out to both wings, he had alienated nearly everyone. 'In politics,' one well-known columnist wrote, 'bipartisan is a death rattle.' Even if the motion failed, ran the general view, the very fact of a vote undermined his authority.

'We'll see about that,' Jim said, and Shirley laughed loudly, as if he had just told a brilliant joke.

He was on his way out to sit by himself and prepare for the next meeting. He gave instructions to Shirley for Simon's resignation letter to be released to the media just before he stepped out into the street to deny to reporters that anything was amiss. Shirley expressed no surprise at her colleague's sacking. Instead, she nodded cheerfully as she gathered up the morning's papers.

It was bad form for all but the PM to be late for a Cabinet meeting. By the time he entered the room, everyone was in place round the table. He took his seat between the chancellor and the foreign secretary. Was he nervous? Not exactly. He was tensed and ready, like a sprinter on the blocks. His immediate concern was to appear plausible. Just as his fingers had known how to knot a tie, so the PM knew that his opening words were best preceded by silence and steady eye contact around the room.

It was in those few seconds, as he met the bland gaze of Trevor Gott, the chancellor of the Duchy of Lancaster, then the home secretary, attorney general, leader of the house, trade, transport, minister without portfolio, that in a startling moment of instant recognition, an unaccustomed, blossoming, transcendent joy swept through him, through his heart and down his spine. Outwardly he remained calm. But he saw it clearly. Nearly all of his Cabinet shared his convictions. Far more important than that, and he had not known this until now, they shared his origins. When he had made his way up Whitehall on that perilous night, he thought he was on a lonely mission. It had never occurred to him that the mighty burden of his task was shared, that others like him were heading towards separate ministries to inhabit other bodies and take up the fight. A couple of dozen, a little swarm of the nation's best, come to inhabit and embolden a faltering leadership.

There was, however, a minor problem, an irritant, an absence. The traitor at his side. He had seen it at a glance. In paradise there was always a devil. Just one. It was likely that among their number there was a brave messenger who had not made it from the palace, who had been sacrificed underfoot, just as he himself almost had, on the pavement outside the gates. When Jim had looked into the eyes of Benedict St John, the foreign secretary, he had come against the blank unyielding wall of a human retina and could go no further. Impenetrable. Nothing there. Merely human. A fake. A collaborator. An enemy of the people. Just the sort who might rebel and vote to bring down his own government. This would have to be dealt with. The opportunity would present itself. Not now.

But here were the rest, and he recognised them instantly through their transparent, superficial human form. A band of brothers and sisters. The metamorphosed radical Cabinet. As they sat round the table, they gave no indication of who they really were, and what they all knew. How eerily they resembled humans! Looking into and beyond the various shades of grey, green, blue and brown of their mammalian eyes, right through to the shimmering blattodean core of their being, he understood and loved his colleagues and their values. They were precisely his own. Bound by iron courage and the will to succeed. Inspired by an idea as pure and thrilling as blood and soil. Impelled towards a goal that lifted beyond mere reason to embrace a mystical sense of nation, of an understanding as simple and as simply good and true as religious faith.

What also bound this brave group was the certainty of deprivation and tears to come, though, to their regret, they would not be their own. But certainty, too, that after victory there would come to the general population the blessing of profound and ennobling self-respect. This room, in this moment, was no place for the weak. The country was about to be set free from a loathsome servitude. From the best, the shackles were already dropping. Soon, the Clockwise incubus would be pitchforked from the nation's back. There are always those who hesitate by an open cage door. Let them cower in elective captivity, slaves to a corrupt and discredited order, their only comfort their graphs and pie-charts, their arid rationality, their pitiful timidity. If only they knew, the momentous event had already slipped from their control, it had moved beyond analysis and debate and into history. It was already unfolding, here at this table. The collective fate was being forged in the heat of the Cabinet's quiet passion. Hard Reversalism was mainstream. Too late to go back!

TWO

The origins of Reversalism are obscure and much in dispute, among those who care. For most of its history, it was considered a thought experiment, an after-dinner game, a joke. It was the preserve of eccentrics, of lonely men who wrote compulsively to the newspapers in green ink. Of the sort who might trap you in a pub and bore you for an hour. But the idea, once embraced, presented itself to some as beautiful and simple. Let the money flow be reversed and the entire economic system, even the nation itself, will be purified, purged of absurdities, waste and injustice. At the end of a working week, an employee hands over money to the company for all the hours that she has toiled. But when she goes to the shops, she is generously compensated at retail rates for every item she carries away. She is forbidden by law to hoard cash. The money she deposits in her bank at the end of a hard day in the shopping mall attracts high negative interest rates. Before her savings are whittled away to nothing, she is therefore wise to go out and find, or train for, a more expensive job. The better, and therefore more costly, the job she finds for herself, the harder she must shop to pay for it. The economy is stimulated, there are more skilled workers, everyone gains. The landlord must tirelessly purchase manufactured goods to pay for his tenants. The government acquires nuclear power stations and expands its space programme in order to send out tax gifts to workers. Hotel managers bring in the best champagne, the softest sheets, rare orchids and the best trumpet player in the best orchestra in town, so that the hotel can afford its guests. The next day, after a successful gig at the dance floor, the trumpeter will have to shop intensely in order to pay for his next appearance. Full employment is the result.

Two significant seventeenth-century economists, Joseph Mun and Josiah Child, made passing references to the reverse circulation of money, but dismissed the idea without giving it much attention. At least, we know the theory was in circulation. There is nothing in Adam Smith's seminal *The Wealth of Nations*, nor in Malthus or Marx. In the late nineteenth century, the American economist Francis Amasa Walker expressed some interest in redirecting the flow of money, but he did so, apparently, in conversation rather than in his considerable writings.

At the crucial Bretton Woods conference in 1944, which framed the post-war economic order and founded the International Monetary Fund, there occurred in one of the sub-committees a fully minuted, impassioned plea for Reversalism by the Paraguayan representative Jesus X. Velasquez. He gained no supporters, but he is generally credited with being the first to use the term in public.

The idea was occasionally attractive in Western Europe to groups on the right or far right, because it appeared to limit the power and reach of the state. In Britain, for example, while the top rate of tax was still eighty-three per cent, the government would have had to hand out billions to the most dedicated shoppers. Keith Joseph was rumoured to have made an attempt to interest Margaret Thatcher in 'reverse-flow economics' but she had no time for it. And in a BBC interview in April 1980, Sir Keith insisted that the rumour was entirely false. Through the nineties, and into the noughties, Reversalism kept a modest profile among various private discussion groups and lesser-known right-of-centre think tanks.

When the Reversalist Party arrived spectacularly on the scene with its populist, anti-elitist message, there were many, even among its opponents, who were already familiar with the 'counter-flow' thesis. After the

Reversalists won the approval of the American president, Archie Tupper, and even more so when it began to lure voters away, the Conservative Party began, in reaction, a slow drift to the right and beyond. But to the Conservative mainstream, Reversalism remained, in the ex-chancellor George Osborne's words, 'the world's daftest idea'. No one knows which economist or journalist came up with the term 'Clockwisers' for those who preferred money to go round in the old and tested manner. Many claimed to have been first.

On the left, especially the 'old left', there was always a handful who were soft on Reversalism. One reason was that they believed it would empower the unemployed. With no jobs to pay for and plenty of time for shopping, the jobless could become seriously rich, if not in hoarded money, then in goods. Meanwhile, the established rich would be able to do nothing with their wealth other than spend it on gainful employment. When working-class Labour voters grasped how much they could earn by getting a son into Eton or a daughter into Cheltenham Ladies' College, they too began to raise their aspirations and defect to the cause.

In order to shore up its electoral support and placate the Reversalist wing of the party, the Conservatives promised in their 2015 election manifesto a referendum on reversing the money flow. The result was the unexpected one, largely due to an unacknowledged alliance between the working poor and the old of all classes. The former had no stake in the status quo and nothing to lose, and they looked forward to bringing home essential goods as well as luxuries, and to being cash rich, however briefly. The old, by way of cognitive dimming, were nostalgically drawn to what they understood to be a proposal to turn back the clock. Both groups, poor and old, were animated to varying degrees by nationalist zeal. In a brilliant coup, the Reversalist press managed to present their cause as a patriotic duty and a promise of national revival and purification: everything that was wrong with the country, including inequalities of wealth and opportunity, the north–south divide and stagnating wages, was caused by the direction of financial flow. If you loved your country and its people, you should upend the existing order. The old flow had merely served the interests of a contemptuous ruling elite. 'Turn the Money Around' became one of many irresistible slogans.

The prime minister who had called the referendum resigned immediately and was never heard of again. In his place there emerged a compromise candidate, the lukewarm Clockwiser James Sams. Fresh from his visit to Buckingham Palace, he promised on the steps of

Downing Street to honour the wish of the people. The money would be turned around. But, as many economists and other commentators had predicted in the low circulation press and unregarded, specialist journals, it was not so easy. The first and overwhelming question concerned overseas trade. The Germans would surely be happy to receive our goods along with our hefty payments. But they would surely not reciprocate by sending their cars to us stuffed with cash. Since we ran a trade deficit, we would soon be broke.

So how was a Reversalist economy to flourish in a Clockwise world? Negotiations with our most important trading partners, the Europeans, stalled. Three years went by. A mostly Clockwise parliament, torn between common sense and bending to the people's will, could offer no practical solutions. Sams had inherited a slim majority and flailed about between passionate factions in his party. Despite that, he was known to some newspapers as Lucky Jim, for it could have been far worse: Horace Crabbe, the leader of the opposition, was himself an elderly Reversalist of the post-Leninist left.

While Sams dithered, and his Cabinet remained divided along several lines of dissent, a purist faction on the Conservative backbenches was hardening its position. Britain must go it alone and convert the rest of the world by example. If the world failed to follow, so much the worse for it. This was ROC. Reversalism in One Country. Then the song and the graffiti were everywhere – Roc around the Clock. We had stood alone before, in 1940, after the fall of France, when German Nazi terror was engulfing Europe. Why bother with their automobiles now? But Sams held back, promising everything to all sides. Most economists, City journalists, business leaders and the entire financial sector predicted economic catastrophe if Sams went the way of the hard Reversalists. Banks, clearing houses, insurance brokers and international corporations were already relocating abroad. Eminent scientists, Nobel laureates, despaired in high-profile letters to the press. But on the street, the popular cry was lusty and heartfelt: get on with it! There was a mood of growing anger, a reasonable suspicion of having been betrayed. A newspaper cartoon depicted Jim Sams as Shakespeare's Gloucester, blinded, teetering on the chalk cliff's edge while Edgar, a tough John Bull Reversalist, urged him to jump.

Then, without warning and to general amazement, Sams and his wavering Cabinet seemed to find their courage. They were about to leap.

*

Once he had seen into all the pairs of eyes round the table, and as soon as he was confident of not bursting into joyful pheromonal song, the prime minister spoke some grave words of welcome. His voice was low and level. A muscle above his right cheekbone twitched repeatedly. No one had seen that before. During his introductory remarks he made a single passing reference to their shared identity when he spoke of this being a 'new' Cabinet which would from now on be voting as one in parliament. No more indiscipline. Blind collective obedience. There followed a sustained rustling and hum of assent around the table. They were of one mind, a colony of dedicated purpose.

Then business. On their way out, they would find copies of a recent survey of voter attitude which they should take away and read closely. They were to be mindful of one particular result: two thirds of those in the twenty-five to thirty-four age group longed for a strong leader who 'did not have to bother with parliament'.

'For now, we do,' Jim said. 'But ...' He let that hang and the room went still. He continued. 'The delayed Reversal Bill comes back to the house in three months. All opposition amendments will be voted down. Adaptation measures will start now. The chancellor will confirm, we'll be spending eight billion on transition arrangements.'

The chancellor, a frosty little fellow with pale grey eyebrows and a white goatee, smothered his moment of surprise and nodded sagely.

The prime minister returned the nod and gave a tight smile that did not part his lips. High reward. 'You should know now. I've fixed Reversalism day, R-Day, for the twenty-fifth of December, when the shops are closed. After that, the Christmas sales will be a colossal boost to GDP.'

He looked around. They were watching him intently. Not a single person doodling on one of the notepads provided. Jim raised his arms and locked his fingers behind his head, a peculiarly pleasant sensation.

'We'll be on course for quantitative easing, printing money so that the department stores can afford their customers and the customers can afford their jobs.'

The foreign secretary said abruptly, 'There's a developing situation in—'

The PM silenced him with a minimal shake of his head. He let his arms fall by his sides. 'Delivering R-Day, or Our Day as we might well call it, is our dedicated first priority. But our second is almost as important. Without it, the first could fail.'

He paused for effect. In that brief interval he had time to consider what to do with Benedict St John. His odd man out. A perfect murder was not easily arranged from Downing Street. One had been planned long ago from the House of Commons by that posturing top-hatted berk, Jeremy Thorpe. How that unravelled was warning enough.

'There'll be some bumps in the road ahead and we have to take the people with us. The focus groups are restive just when we need to be wildly popular. Vitally important. So, we'll be raising taxes for the low paid and lowering them for the rich. Big handouts for the workers after the twenty-fifth. To pay for that, as I'm sure our wise chancellor will agree, we'll increase government revenues by employing another twenty thousand policemen, fifty thousand nurses, fifteen thousand doctors and two hundred thousand dustmen to ensure daily collections. With their tax breaks, these new hires should easily be able to pay for their jobs. And the Chinese owe us eight hundred billion for the three nuclear power stations they'll be building.'

The attentive silence in the room appeared to shift, to downgrade in quality. No one trusted the Chinese government. Would they pay up? Would they put their own vast economy into reverse? Someone coughed politely. A few were examining their fingernails. If he had not quite lost the Cabinet's support, Jim realised he was in danger of earning its scepticism. He was saved by the minister for transport, an affable, pipe-smoking MP for a north-eastern constituency, believed to be fanatically ambitious.

'We'd save a lot of money by pressing ahead with the high-speed rail link to Birmingham.'

'Brilliant. Thank you, Jane.'

Emboldened, the muscular, square-jawed minister of defence Humphrey Batton said, 'And by commissioning four more aircraft carriers.'

'Excellent, Humph.'

'Ten thousand new prison places would bring in two and a half billion.'

'Well done, Frank.'

Suddenly, they were all at it, anxious to please, talking over each other by calling out departmental projects enabled by the new dispensation.

The PM sat back, beaming, letting the voices wash over him, occasionally murmuring, 'Jolly good ... that's the spirit ... tops!'

Inevitably, after a while, a feeling of exhaustion descended on the room, and into this lull the foreign secretary spoke.

'What about us?'

All heads turned respectfully towards Benedict St John. In that moment Jim realised that he was the only one who understood the man's unique status.

'What?'

The foreign secretary spread his palms to indicate an obvious point. 'Take my own case. But it could be yours. Next year I'm supposed to be in every capital in the world for Global Britain, persuading governments to come in with us. And I'm on a salary of £141,405 a year.'

'So?'

'With all my extended family responsibilities, it's simply too much to live on. How am I going to find time to do all the shopping to afford my job?'

Again, there was that quiet rustling sound beneath the table. Jim glanced around the room. Was Benedict being satirical? Perhaps he had spoken for all of them.

The prime minister stared at him in full contempt. 'Bloody hell, how should I ... you just, er ...'

It was the transport minister, Jane Fish, who once more helped him out.

'Go on Amazon, Bennie. One click. Get yourself a Tesla!'

A general sigh of relief at this elegant solution. The PM was ready to move on, but St John had not finished.

'I'm worried. On your R-Day the pound is likely to take a dive.'

Your? This was intolerable, but the PM managed a kindly look. 'That'll help our imports.'

'Exactly my point. Exports. We'll have to send even more money abroad.'

Jim explained as though to a child. 'Balanced by money we earn from imports.'

'In three years St Kitts and Nevis is all we have. Jim, this could be ruinous.'

Every minister was watching closely this direct challenge. The prime minister's sudden delighted laughter was genuine, for he had seen ahead, not only to the foreign secretary's inexplicable death, but to his funeral, a medium-grand affair at which Jim himself would deliver the peroration. St Paul's. Elgar's 'Nimrod'. The Horse Guards. Which reminded him, he had not yet had breakfast.

'Well, Benedict, as Karl Marx said, there's a lot of ruin in a nation.'

'It was Adam Smith.'

'All the truer for that.'

The ministers relaxed. They were disposed to take this last as a clincher, as a crushing remark. Jim drew breath to announce the next item.

But the foreign secretary said, 'Now to the important matter.'

'For God's sake, man,' the home secretary, Frank Corde, growled.

Benedict was sitting opposite the minister of defence. When the two men exchanged a glance, Batton shrugged and looked down at his hands. You tell them.

'It's a developing situation. No official statements as yet. But I'm told that the *Daily Mail* is about to run it on its website. So you all should know. I'm not usually—'

'Get on with it,' Jim said.

'Just after seven this morning a French frigate collided with the *Larkin*, one of our fishing boats off the Brittany coast, near Roscoff. Cut it in two. Crew of six. All pulled out of the drink.'

'Glad to hear it. So let's—'

'All drowned.'

The prime minister and his colleagues had grown up with death as a daily feature, with customary posthumous feasting as a hygienic necessity, as well as being a rather decent— he wrenched his thoughts away. He knew enough to allow a short silence before saying, 'Tragic. But things happen at sea. Why are we discussing this?'

'The boat was fishing illegally. In French coastal waters.'

'Well?'

The foreign secretary rested his chin on his hands. 'We were keeping this quiet while the relatives were being informed. But it broke on Twitter. The story going around now is the French rammed our boat deliberately. Enforcing their territorial rights.'

The chancellor of the Duchy of Lancaster said, 'What's the French line?'

'Thick fog, smallish wooden boat, two kilometres offshore, transponder off for some reason. Didn't show on the frigate's radar. Our own naval data and other sources back up everything they're saying.'

'That's clear enough, then,' the attorney general said.

The foreign secretary looked at his watch. 'The *Mail* will be running a fighting piece this morning on their website. Patriotically outraged. Soon the story will be on all platforms. It's getting nasty. Fifty minutes ago, just as we were sitting down, someone put a brick through a window at the French embassy.'

He paused and looked at the prime minister. 'We need a statement from the highest level. Take the heat out of this nonsense.'

They all looked at Jim, who tipped back in his chair and said to the ceiling, 'Hmm.'

In a coaxing tone, Benedict added, 'Plus a call to the French president, with the conversation put on the record?'

'Hmm.'

They watched and waited.

At last he righted his chair and nodded at the Cabinet secretary, who customarily sat apart. 'If they're being buried together I want to be at the funeral.'

The foreign secretary started to say, 'That might seem a bit—'

'Hang on. Better than that. If the coffins are coming back together, and bloody well make sure they are, I intend to be there, quayside, airstrip, whatever.'

While the rest were frozen, not so much in outrage as fascination, the foreign secretary was trembling. He seemed to be about to stand, then sat again. 'Jim. You cannot do that.'

The prime minister appeared suddenly joyful. He adopted a breezy, mocking, see-saw voice. 'Now, Benedict, when this meeting breaks up, you're to go round the corner to your splendid office and do two things. You'll summon the French ambassador and demand an explanation. And you'll tell your press office what you're doing.'

The foreign secretary took a deep breath. 'We can't play games. This is a very close ally.'

'Six of our brave men have died. Until it's proved otherwise, I'm assuming this was a despicable assault.'

Finally, the secretary of state for defence found his courage. His voice had a throttled sound. 'Actually, the Admiralty data is pretty sound.'

'Admirals! Time servers, the lot of them. No doubt with farmhouses in the Dordogne to consider.'

This was good. Such an unfashionable English corner of France. There were chuckles round the table. The tight line of St John's jaw suggested he had nothing more to say. But the prime minister went on staring hard at him for almost thirty seconds. The effect on the rest was intimidating, in particular on Humphrey Batton, popular in the country for having once been a captain in the Second Paras. He found something of interest in his water glass on the table in front of him. He clasped it tightly between both hands.

'We'll get the Americans on side,' Jim said. 'They have special feelings for the French. Comments? Good. Now, moving on.' He took from his pocket a scrap of paper torn out from the *Spectator* magazine. On it was a pencilled list. 'To mark R-Day we'll mint a commemorative ten-pound coin. My idea is for a mirror image of a clock.'

'Brilliant ... wonderful idea,' was the collective response. The chancellor swallowed hard and nodded. Someone said, 'On the reverse, I assume.'

The prime minister glared about, looking for the culprit. The joke fell flat. 'Any other thoughts?'

There were none.

'Next. We'll institute an R-Day national holiday. The Christmas period's no good, obviously, so I'm going for the nearest date in the new year, January the second. Objections?'

'No,' they murmured.

'Good. That happens to be my birthday.'

At that, the entire Cabinet, except for the foreign secretary, applauded with slaps to the table.

Modestly, the prime minister held up a restraining hand and the room fell silent. In his short, previous existence he had never known such contentment. It seemed to him five years had passed, not three or four hours, since he had woken, sad and deranged, unable to control his limbs or even his tongue. He saw it in his colleagues' faces – he was in command, he was a force, here and in the land, and beyond. Hard to believe. Thrilling. Amazing. Nothing could stand in his way.

He glanced down at his list. 'Ah yes. I had this thought. The Reversalist movement needs a song, a positive one. An anthem of some sort. Something more with-it than "Ode to Joy". And it came to me. This old favourite from the sixties. "Walking Back to Happiness." You must know it. No? For God's sake, Helen Shapiro!'

They didn't know it, or her. But they did not dare shake their heads. Whatever secretly bound them, they were now immersed, lost to their respective roles. The cost of their ignorance was high, for the prime minister began to sing in a wavering baritone, with his arms spread wide and a forced grin like a practised crooner.

'Walking back to happiness, woopah oh yeah yeah.'

Nor did they dare catch each other's eye. They sensed that a misplaced smile could terminate a career. Nor, when the PM made a come hither wiggle with his fingers, did they dare not join the chorus. They sang in solemn unison 'Yay yay yay yay ba dum be do' as they might a hymn by Hubert Parry.

Even while in full throat, Jim saw that the foreign secretary was silent. Not even mouthing the words. He was staring straight ahead, immobile, perhaps with embarrassment. Or was it contempt?

When the singing came to a ragged end, St John stood and said to no one in particular, 'Well, I have things to do, as you know.' Without acknowledging the PM, he quickly left the room.

As he turned to watch him go, Jim was amazed at how it was possible to feel such joy and such hatred at the same time. A human heart, of which he was now in full possession, was a wondrous thing.

*

After he had brought the meeting to an end, Jim spent some minutes alone, working on his priorities statement. He gave some selected quotations to Shirley to shape into a press release. She worked quickly and well. By the time word came that his car was outside and the front door was opening for him, the press already had wind of something new and bold sweeping through his government. How fine it was to step out into daylight, to tower above the threshold he had crawled over the night before. Fine too, to hear the babble of excited questions shouted at him from the other side of the street. He paused by the front door, which had closed behind him, to give the photographers their half minute, but he did not speak. Instead, he raised a hand in friendly salute and gave the cameras a determined half smile. He was completely in command now of his binocular, non-mosaic, high-colour focused gaze, and he let it move slowly over the faces of the journalists, over the lenses, and then, as the Jaguar XJ Sentinel (an armoured car much to his taste) drew up and the door opened, he raised both hands in triumph, now grinning broadly, and stooped to slip onto the rear seat.

On the short ride down Whitehall to the Palace of Westminster, he had time to relish the moment ahead when he would stand at the despatch box to make the intentions of his government clear. What stirred him was the thought of the hidden, silent audience crouching behind the wainscoting. Even now they would be amassing in the darkness. How proud of him his family would be.

*

From *Hansard*, 19 September, Vol. 663 Priorities for Government

The Prime Minister (James Sams)

With permission, Mr Speaker, I shall make a statement on the mission of what is, in effect, a new Conservative government. When the bill returns to this house, Mr Speaker, our mission will be to deliver Reversalism for the purpose of uniting and re-energising our great country and not only making it great again, but making it the greatest place on earth. By 2050 it is more than possible, and less than impossible, that the UK will be the greatest and most prosperous economy in Europe. We will lie at the centre of a new network of reverse-flow trade deals. We will be the best on the planet in all fields. We will be the earth's home of the electric airplane. We will lead the world in not wrecking our precious planet. That same world will follow our shining example and every nation will reverse its money flow in order not to be left behind—*[Interruption.]*

Mr Speaker

Order. There is far too much noise in this Chamber. Too many members think it is all right for them to shout out their opinions at the prime minister. Let us be clear: it is not.

The Prime Minister

Mr Speaker, I applaud your intervention. This government is no longer divided. Myself and all the ministers are one body and we speak with one mind. We are formidable in our unity. The Bill will therefore pass. Nothing will stand in our way. We are turbocharging the civil service to prepare for the transition. We will move swiftly to accelerate and extend our trade deals beyond brave St Kitts and Nevis. Until that time, we proclaim

Reversalism in One Country. We will stand alone just as we have stood alone in the past. A lot of negativity about Reversalism has been wildly overdone. This is no time for faint Clockwise thinking. Let no one doubt it, the money flow is about to change direction – and about time, too. On day one, on R-Day, the beneficial effects will be felt on both macro and micro levels. On R-Day, for example, our newly empowered police might pull over a recklessly speeding motorist and hand through the window two fifty-pound notes. It will be that driver's responsibility, in the face of possible criminal charges, to use that money to work and pay for more overtime, or find a slightly better job. This is just one example, Mr Speaker, of how Reversalism will stimulate the economy, incentivise our brilliant citizens, and render our democracy more robust.

Reversalism will bless our future – clean, green, prosperous, united, confident and ambitious. When, together, we bend our sinews to the task, the dead hand of Clockwise economics and its vast bureaucracy of enterprise-denying rules and Health and Safety impediments will be lifted from us, all of us, one by one. And very soon, it will be lifted from all the nations on earth. We stand at the beginning of a golden age. Mr Speaker,

I commend this future to the house just as much as I commend this statement.

Several hon. Members rose—

Mr Speaker

Order.

[Continues.]

THREE

The youth who threw the brick at the French embassy that morning ran off and no arrest was made. This was noted in Paris. At the time of the incident, the crowd in Knightsbridge was estimated at around fifty. By late afternoon there were more than five hundred, some of whom were trawlermen who had travelled from Hull in buses laid on by the Reversalist Party. There were chants and shouts, but otherwise it was a peaceful demonstration. The five extra policemen drafted in had little to do but stand by the main doors of the embassy and watch. But just after four thirty someone threw 'an incendiary device'. It landed harmlessly on the damp grass by some laurels under a window and did not ignite. It was a milk bottle containing an inch or so of lighter fluid. It was reported as a petrol bomb, which may have been technically correct. This attack was also noted in Paris.

Earlier that afternoon, the French ambassador, Le Comte Henri de Clermont L'Hérault, was summoned to the Foreign and Commonwealth Office to account for the deaths of the six English trawlermen. The meeting was officially described as 'constructive', with the ambassador expressing sincere and heartfelt condolences to the families and profoundest apologies for the tragic accident. Little of this was picked up by the press, for the prime minister came out of Downing Street at 5 p.m. and made a statement of untypical resolve. The so-called bomb, deplorable as it was, had been examined and was a firework, in fact, 'a damp squib', and likely nothing more than a joke in extremely poor taste. Then Sams read out the names of the dead men, whom he described as 'English heroes'. He too expressed deepest condolences to the bereaved families and said that he was 'disturbed' by this tragic incident and was 'not wholly satisfied' with the explanations given by the ambassador earlier. The PM had heard expert advice. Modern technology, especially on an up-to-date naval vessel, was such that it was hard to understand how a thirty-foot fishing boat could not be detected in a fog, however thick. He understood that the skipper of the boat might not have known that he was inside French territorial waters and that he was fishing illegally. Sams accepted that in a rules-based international order, territorial rights must be respected. However – and here he paused – where violations occur, 'responses must be considered and appropriate'. He was therefore 'seeking further clarification from our very good friends, the French'. Refusing questions, he abruptly turned away and went back inside Number Ten.

In an instant, out of tragedy a diplomatic crisis was born. President Larousse, already baffled and irritated by *l'inversion britannique* and the disruption it threatened to French exports of wine and cheese to the UK, was, his spokesman said, 'disappointed' that the English should 'doubt the word of a very good friend'. That the Sams administration should imply that it was French government policy to 'murder innocent fishermen who wandered into our coastal waters was an insult to all that France holds dear'. Clearly, M. Sams, in difficulties over a decision that had divided his country, was positioning himself behind 'a nationalist wave of manufactured anger fed by an irrational Twitter storm'. Reluctantly, the president had decided to recall his ambassador. Le Comte Henri de Clermont L'Hérault would be returning to Paris for consultations.

Reasonably enough, Jim decided to recall the British ambassador in Paris. Things were shaping up well. In a difficult time such as this, the country needed a staunch enemy. Patriotic journalists praised the prime minister for facing down the French and speaking up for 'our lost boys'. The priorities statement to the Commons had also gone down well with important sections of the press. An opinion piece in the *Mail* was headlined, 'Who Put the Fire in Jim's Belly?'

At the end of that first, crowded day, the prime minister had retreated to his small apartment at the top of the building and busied himself with understanding Twitter, a primitive version, so he decided, of the pheromonal unconscious. He read Archie Tupper's recent output and began to suspect that the American president was, just possibly, 'one of us'. An obsequious fellow sent by a Whitehall IT team helped the PM open his own account. Within two hours he had 150,000 followers. An hour later, that number had doubled.

While he stretched out on the sofa, Jim found that a tweet was the perfect medium in which to reflect sagely on the Roscoff Affair, as it was now known. His first attempt was feebly derivative. 'Clockwiser Larousse is just a loser, and in my view the least effective French President in living memory.' *In my view* – as if there were others. Limp. And no calling it back. The following day the American president was awake early to head the debate from his bed and demonstrate how it was done. 'Tiny Sylvie Larousse sinking English ships. BAD!' It was poetry, smoothly combining density of meaning with fleet-footed liberation from detail. Larousse was emasculated, then diminished with a taunt that, true or not (his name was Sylvain, he was five foot nine), must forever be his badge; the fisherman's boat became a ship, the ship became ships; no tedious mention of the dead. The final judgement was childlike and pure, memorable and monosyllabically correct. And the parting flourish of those caps, that laconic exclamation mark! From the land of the free, here was a lesson in imaginative freedom.

Later, with pencil poised over notepad, Jim considered some refinements to the Reversalism Bill. He could see opportunities for criminals. Be unemployed, shop relentlessly, stuff a suitcase with cash, hop abroad to some dirty EU economy, open a bank account. Work to earn in Calais, shop to earn in Dover. Bastards. The solution was clear – it was happening anyway. The cashless society would create a digital trail for every pound earned in the shops, and every pound spent on work. Hoarding sums above twenty-five pounds would be a criminal offence, well advertised. Maximum sentence? Best not to be too harsh, not at first. So, five years.

He wrote notes at high speed in a neat copperplate, taking pleasure in forming the letters. An opposable thumb was not such a bad idea. Upstart young species like *Homo sapiens* sometimes came up with a useful development. As for the elaboration or broadcast of ideas, writing, despite its artisanal charm, was lugubriously analogue. He paused only once from his labours to devour a plate of parmigiana brought to him on a tray. He didn't bother with the salad.

Next. As soon as the bill was passed, his immediate concern must be to persuade the Americans to reverse their economy. From that, everything would follow. The Chinese would have to reverse in order to be able to afford their exports, so would Japan and the Europeans. Getting Tupper on board needed forethought, nice treats. Jim was on his fourth pages of notes. *Problem: AT not drinker/state visit softener/banquet with HM gold carriage flunkeys fanfares address parliament etc/Most Nob Order of Garter plus Vic Cross plus hon. knighthd/memship White's/gift Hyde Park as priv golf course.*

But the American president was a serious man of big tastes, with his own moral certitudes, by background not trained up to value the subtle ribbons-and-medals allure of the honours system. What were White's or Hyde Park to one who owned more expensive clubs and bigger courses? Who cared for 'Sir' when one was 'Mr President' for life? In the late afternoon of that day, the prime minister had given the matter some serious thought. He had set his staff to research certain legal niceties of the American system, and the extent of presidential power and how both might fare in a reverse-flow economy. Jim now had all he needed to know about article two of the US constitution. He was aware of the force of law and astonishing reach of a presidential executive order. Like most people, he already knew that the president was also the commander-in-chief of the United States Armed Forces. The Cabinet Office had provided Jim with a general overview of the process by which the American defence budget was negotiated and effected. He had in his notes the precise figure in billions of dollars for the year ahead. The attorney general had come to Downing Street to explain the position. The US president could, by his own order, devolve the defence budget as agreed by congress, to his own office. By standard Reversalist processes, funds would flow back up the system, from the army, navy and air force personnel, and all their suppliers and all the manufacturers, directly to the president. Seven hundred and sixteen billion dollars would be his

'Personally his? Legally his?' Jim had asked the attorney general.

'Legally, yes. It would set a precedent that might surprise his opponents. But with this president, most people have grown accustomed to surprises.'

'Let me be clear,' Jim said. 'He could bank that money?'

'Of course. Cayman Islands, perhaps. The Russian president should be able to help. Even at low interest rates he could live reasonably well on seven or eight billion a year without touching the capital.'

'What about US defences?'

The attorney general laughed. 'Congress would ratify the budget again. These days, they love borrowing money.'

But now, as Big Ben up the road sounded a dolorous eleven o' clock, Jim worried how he would pitch this on the phone. Tupper was not one for the simple life. Would 716 billion do it? Should he suggest the president appropriate the education budget? Along with healthcare? But that might require three executive orders. Too complicated. He would have to take a chance. It was 6 p.m. in Washington. The president would be busy watching television and might not appreciate the interruption. Jim hesitated a few more seconds, staring into the swirl of encrusted colour, purplish reds and creamy whites, on his empty dinner plate, then phoned down to tell the night staff to put through an unminuted call.

It took them twenty-five minutes to exchange identification protocols, enable the voice scrambling encryption, and get the president's attention, and another ten to patch him through. Not bad for an unscheduled conference.

'Jim.'

'Mr President. I hope I'm not disturbing you in the middle of important—'

'No, just, um ... I hear you're sticking it to the French.'

'They murdered six of our lads.'

'Murder isn't good, Jim.'

'Absolutely. I couldn't agree more.'

For an anxious moment their accord drained the exchange of purpose. Jim could hear down the line shouts and pistol shots in the background and the neighing of many horses, then a sudden change of scene, expansive orchestral music with French horns and strings, suggestive of open desert with cacti and buttes. He cast around for safe small talk. 'How is Mel—'

But the president spoke over him. 'What's the latest with, you know, that thing, the Revengelism project?'

'Reversalism? Fantastic. We're almost ready to go. Great excitement over here. It's a historical turning point.'

'Shake things up is good. Give the EU a bad time.'

'Mr President, this is what I wanted to discuss with you.'

'You got two minutes.'

So the prime minister laid out the matter in the terms his attorney general had used, adding some colourful plumbing and weather imagery of his own. Up the pipes came a counterflow surge of newly released energy that explosively blew old thinking, blasted old blockages aside and at the end, the release point or outlet, there shot up high into the air a fabulous fountain of trade deals and also funds, electronic dollars that fell earthwards like longed-for rain, like a storm of spiralling autumn leaves, like a vortex-blizzard of snowflakes pouring down into ...

'My account?' the president said in a husky voice. 'You're saying into my business account?'

'Offshore, of course. You should get your own people to check.'

A silence, broken only by the rippling sound of TV laughter, and of a honky-tonk piano and the clinking of glasses, and celebratory gunfire.

Finally, 'When you put it that way I can see there might be something in it. Definitely. I think together we could make Revengelism work, Jim. But now I've got to, um ...'

'One last thing, Mr President. May I ask you something personal?'

'Sure. As long as it's not about—'
'No, no. Of course. It's about ... *before*.'
'Before what, Jim?'
'Six?'
'Say again.'
'All right. Are you ... Did you once ...'
'Once what?'
'Have, erm ...'
'Jesus! Get it out, Jim! Have what?'
It came in a whisper. 'Six legs?'
The line went dead.

*

The weather, that dependable emblem of private and national mood, was in turmoil. A five-day, record-breaking heatwave was followed by two weeks of record-breaking rain across the entire country. Like all the lesser rivers, the Thames rose, and Parliament Square languished under four inches of water and much floating plastic and waxed-cardboard detritus. The best photographers could not make the scene picturesque. As soon as the rains stopped, a tall heat strode in from the Azores once more and a second, longer heatwave began. For a week, as the floodwaters receded, there was thick smooth silt underfoot everywhere in riverine London. The humidity never fell below ninety per cent. When the mud dried, there was dust. When the scorching winds blew, which they did with unusual ferocity and for days on end, there were novel urban sandstorms, brownish yellow, thick enough to obscure from view Nelson on his column. Some of the sand, it turned out on analysis, came from the Sahara. A live black scorpion four inches long was found in a consignment of fresh dates on sale in Borough Market. It was impossible to persuade feverish social media that these venomous creatures were not wind-born, and had not breezed in from north Africa on a south-westerly. A deluge of scorpions had biblical echoes. Real or not, they added to the profound unease among the substantial minority of the electorate convinced that a catastrophe was at hand, driven by a government of reckless ideologues. Another substantial minority, slightly larger, believed that a great adventure was at hand. It could hardly wait for it to start. Both factions were represented in parliament, though not in government. The weather was right. Turmoil and reduced visibility was everywhere.

Unhelpfully, the French released the dead fishermen in their coffins one by one, after post mortems, over a week. They were flown to Stansted, not the sort of airport Jim wished to be seen in. The dead, at government insistence, were not released immediately to the families. Instead, they were held in cold storage outside Cambridge and when the last man had been brought in from France, all six were flown to Royal Wootton Bassett by an RAF transport plane. Jim took charge of the planning. He decided that there would be no brass band. Instead, he would stand alone on the airstrip, silently facing a camera crew and the massive four-engine propeller plane as it taxied to a stop. A brave lonely figure confronting the giant machine. Jim's antennae were finely attuned to public sentiment. As it happened, it was the first day of the heavy rains. The coffins, draped in Union Jacks, were brought out in single file, by members of the Grenadier Guards, marching in funereal slow step, and placed at the prime minister's feet. The rain played well. He correctly refused an umbrella as he stood to attention in the downpour. Were those tears on his face? It was reasonable to think so. The nation came together in a passing frenzy of grief. In Hull and near HMS *Belfast* in London, flowers, teddy bears and toy fishing boats were piled forty feet high.

Then came the second heatwave. Tucked under a baking roof, its windows shut tight against the gritty winds, the prime minister's apartment warmed to an extraordinary level. But Jim was energised by the moist heat. He had never felt healthier. His blood, excited and thinned, raced through and nourished his busy mind with fresh ideas. He had refused to replace Simon with a new special adviser. He had also dispensed with Cabinet meetings. Delivering Reversal was his only purpose, to which his every sinew was bent, just as he had promised in parliament. Reversalism consumed him and he no longer knew why or how. He entered a state of barely conscious bliss, unaware of time or hunger or even his own identity. He was deliriously obsessed, burning with strange passion, hot with impatient desire for explanations, details, revisions. Prompted by a dim recollection of Churchill in 1940, he appended to every written directive, 'Report back to me today to confirm the above has been accomplished.' These words were made available to the press. The prime minister took meetings with the heads of MI5 and 6, business and trade union leaders, doctors, nurses, farmers, headmasters, prison governors and university vice chancellors. Preferring not to take questions, he patiently explained how their different sectors would blossom in the new regime. He had regular consultations with the chief whip. It looked like the Reversalism Bill would pass easily with a margin of twenty votes or so. The PM wrote memos, issued commands, and made motivating phone calls to his ministerial team. He sent down inspirational press statements to Shirley. The civil service was now properly turbocharged; across London the lights were on all night in the ministries. And in the Downing Street apartment too. Outside, by day and night, dispatch riders lined up to collect or deliver documents too confidential to be entrusted to digital transfer.

Developments further afield were also good. A British-owned farmhouse in Provence was daubed with red paint by French patriots. The London tabloids were healthily inflamed. When the prime minister held President Larousse personally accountable, the figure of a club-wielding John Bull with Jim's face appeared in a *Sun* cartoon and was widely circulated on the Internet. In the polls, Sams was up fifteen points over Horace Crabbe. In his early morning tweets, the American president described Prime Minister Sams as 'a great man' and announced that it was time to reverse the entire US economy. Before lunch, a thousand points were wiped off the Dow Jones. The next morning, Tupper changed his mind. He was, he said, just 'playing with the idea'. Stock markets around the world were reassured. When the chairman of the Federal Reserve dismissed Reversalism as 'loopy', the President doubled back in anger. Reversalism was on again. It would bring 'the old elite to its knees'. This time the Dow Jones was untroubled. As one Wall Street insider said, the markets would panic when it was time to panic.

It was Gloria, the young woman in the trouser suit who had come to wake Jim on that first morning, who tapped on the door late one evening to deliver the news. Simon had been found hanged by a towrope in the bedroom of his house in Ilford, where he lived alone. Even better, there was no note. He had been dead for at least a week. While Gloria went down to find some champagne, Jim wrote a quick note of praise and regret. It was good of Simon not to be writing a memoir or plotting with enemies of the Project. Gloria said her goodnight and took the warm encomium – deeply moving, everyone would say – downstairs for Shirley to type up and send out. The prime minister drank the bottle alone while he continued with his work. But his usual concentration was just a little diminished. Something was nagging at him, a little uncoiling thread of suspicion that he couldn't quite justify. At last, he had to put down his pen to think this through. It came down to nothing more than trivial superstition that he, the most rational of creatures, could not dismiss: there had been nothing but good news lately – the exhilarating pace of work, the chief whip's calculations, the collapse of the 1922 Committee revolt, the dead fishermen, his press, his soaring popularity, the red paint, Tupper's praise and now this. Was he being so unreasonable when the experience of a lifetime demonstrated that any torrent of delightful fortune must at some point be checked? At the end of his rope, Simon had made the prime minister nervous. He slept poorly, worrying all night that this happy death presaged a turning point.

And so it did, the next morning, not one point but two, each turning in the same direction. The first came in the form of an early morning email from the chief whip. There was a secret cabal among his own backbenchers, a group of Clockwisers who had been meeting in a private house somewhere outside London. Not much was known about them, their numbers or their names. There were obvious candidates, but no evidence, only bland denials. They had voted with the government so far to conceal their identities. It was a mystery or a miracle, the way they had dodged the attentions of the whips' office. But one thing was now known for sure. The foreign secretary, Benedict St John, was the moving force and it was suspected that the intention was to help the opposition defeat the Reversalism Bill when it came back to the Commons.

This ugly disloyalty was on the PM's mind as he shaved and dressed and descended the stairs. In his fury, he wanted to hit someone, or break something. It was an effort to appear pleasant when his junior staff greeted him in the hallway. He had been too preoccupied, too complacent. He should have dealt with Benedict St John days ago. If only he was a free agent, Jim would happily have taken an axe to the man's throat. These furious, violent thoughts did not begin to fade until he sat down to his coffee and his tight-lipped press secretary laid before him the *Daily Telegraph*'s double-page spread.

It was one of those leaks from within the heart of government in which the paper excelled, hardly seeming to care how this one went against the grain of its strict Reversalist line. The allure of a scoop was total. This was a well-laid-out reduction of a Royal Navy memo that revealed the Roscoff Affair to have been an accident. It was hard to doubt it: radar and satellite data, ship-to-shore intercepts, rescue divers to frigate intercepts, French embassy and Élysée Palace intercepts, and eye-witness reports. Jim read it over twice. Nothing here that Simon could ever have had access to. Among the many diagrams and photographs was a picture of himself, rain-sodden and erect on the airfield tarmac by the flag-covered coffins. The leak was a political calculation, and clearly a Clockwise-inspired attack. The source was obvious. These two bad developments were related. His enemies were on the move and Reversalism was under threat. Jim knew he had to act quickly.

Shirley's office had already prepared a press statement. Jim read it through, deleting all hints of apology to the French. It was a decent holding position. He was giving no interviews. Essentially, the prime minister was immensely relieved to hear that what happened to the crew of the *Larkin* was the consequence of a tragic accident. Here, from our courageous Royal Navy, was the irrefutable proof that the French government, for reasons of their own, had been unable to provide. The terrible loss suffered by the families of the lost crew remained a matter of deep, etc... bereaved, etc. The prime minister thanked the French authorities for all their etc., etc., and wished to reassure our good neighbour that routine intercepts of their radio and telephone traffic was no more than a sincere expression of the UK's profound esteem. Etc., etc., etc., for the Fifth Republic.

He signed off on the text and, on his way back upstairs, told his staff that he was not to be disturbed. In the apartment he locked the door, cleared papers from the coffee table and placed at its centre a large notepad and a red ink biro. He sat, hesitating, chin in hand, then began to write names, draw circles round them, link the circles with single or double lines embellished with arrows and question marks. He appraised actions and their possible consequences, their discoverability and their deniablity through the distorting prism of alliances, rupture and disgrace. His was a perfectly pitched and balanced mind, well adapted by inheritance over unimaginable stretches of time to the art of survival and the advancement of his kind. Also, a life of constant, almost routine struggle had perfected in him effortless mastery in defending all that he possessed – while seeming not to. He was calm in the knowledge that he would prevail. And in this moment of scheming, he was richly self-aware, fully alive to the joy of politics at its purest, which was the pursuit of ends at all costs. He thought and calculated hard, and after half an hour it was clear to him that it was too late to commission the foreign secretary's murder. He turned to a fresh blank page, and considered.

There were other, gentler forms of murder. Contemporary social life was a metaphorical armoury of newly purposed weapons, of tripwires, poisoned darts, land mines waiting for a careless step. This time Jim did not hesitate. It took him two hours to write his article, possibly for the *Guardian*, a confession of sorts that demanded of its author the trick, entirely alien to him, of inhabiting another's mind. He persevered and within three paragraphs was already beginning to feel sorry for himself, or for the self he would have to find and cajole. Or threaten. It was an open-ended scheme. Only by writing it could it be discovered. When he was done, he walked up and down within the confined attic space in a state of exultation. There was nothing more liberating than a closely knit sequence of lies. So this was why people became writers. Then he sat again with his hand hovering near the phone. There were three names on his list. Whom could he trust? Or, whom did he mistrust the least? Even as he set himself the question he knew the answer, and his forefinger was already tapping the keys.

*

The one thing everybody knew about Jane Fish was that she smoked a pipe. Everybody also knew that, actually, she didn't. She wasn't even a smoker. Years ago, starting out in the humblest, most wretched, least popular job in government, secretary of state for Northern Ireland, she had attended an event in Belfast for an anti-smoking charity. She agreed to take one puff on a pipe and blow the smoke into the face of a child to highlight the dangers of secondary smoking. The little girl's eyes were closed and she did not inhale. But public life is lived in broad strokes. The customary two-day media storm followed. Since Fish was outspoken and often in the news and had a pleasant, unexceptional face, cartoonists had no choice but to keep the pipe in her mouth. For political sketch writers, she would be forever 'pipe-smoking Jane Fish'. She was popular. In the spectrum of available opinion, she belonged mostly in the no-nonsense faction and was well liked for her stand against breastfeeding in public. She had been a passionate Clockwiser until, respectful of the will of the people, she became a passionate Reversalist. She was admired for speaking well for both.

Of the three women on his list, she was, in the prime minister's view, the closest to her pheromonal roots. His judgement was good. On the phone that night, when he laid out the facts, she understood immediately the need for firm action. She confided that she'd always had her doubts about Benedict. Jim had his hand-written article biked round to her immediately in a sealed pouch. She phoned back ninety minutes later with her suggested changes. Some concerned matters of historical detail, others were what she called 'a matter of voice'. The following morning, Shirley typed up the messy manuscript and went round to King's Cross to deliver it to and negotiate with the editor of the *Guardian*. The prime minister had insisted that the press secretary was to remain on the premises while the piece went into production. This was a broad-minded paper that had once run a column on its opinion pages by Osama bin Laden, and employed as a journalist a paid-up member of Hizb ut-Tahrir, an extremist organisation. It was a bit of a stretch to run a piece by Jane Fish, but how could a Clockwise paper resist when one minister was destroying another in a government it despised?

It is a wonderful sight, deeply stirring, when a great newspaper has only a few hours to get behind an important story. Immense expertise and teamwork, long memories and rapid analysis come nobly into play. The whole building hums. Shirley told her staff later that it was like being in a frontline hospital at the height of a bloody battle. The entire front page was turned around, along with three pages inside, and a leader by the editor herself. By five that afternoon, the first copies were coming off the presses. That may have been a high moment for older journalists, to hold a fresh hard copy in their hands. But it was irrelevant. By then, the paper's website had been running the revelations, with constant updates, for four hours. Plenty of time for rival papers to pick up the story for tomorrow's editions, and for evening television news to rejig their running orders. Social media, blogs, political webzines were on fire. The Roscoff Affair, with its niggling historical details of murders that turned out to have been mere accidents, drifted down the lists. If the prime minister had pointed the finger at the French, he was only as mistaken as everyone else. No skulduggery off the Brittany coast, but plenty here in Whitehall. A holder of one of the great offices of state was in disgrace. Where was the foreign secretary? When was he going to resign? How would the government handle the crisis? What did this mean for Reversalism? When were powerful men going to reform their ways? To this last, the prime minister had a single-word answer.

FOUR

It was 2,857 words long, and written more in regret than vengefulness. This was a tale of harassment, bullying, obscene taunts and inappropriate touching that led by turns to verbal abuse. That Fish went out of her way to stress that no actual rape took place gave her account added veracity. That the blunt, plain-speaking northerner should relate these matters with such raw sensitivity moved some to tears. Even a subeditor was wet-eyed. The appalling events related to a twenty-month period fifteen years before, when Jane Fish was parliamentary private secretary to Benedict St John and he was minister for work and pensions. She had suffered ever since, too fearful for her career, too humiliated to speak out and strangely protective of her gifted colleague. She was breaking silence now because the foreign secretary's youngest child was eighteen and because she had come to believe she had a duty to younger women who occupied vulnerable positions like the one she once had. The front page headline was, 'Foreign Secretary's Shame'. A contemporary photograph showed Fish following St John onto a train, carrying his luggage. Around the body of the piece were boxed texts of explanation and analysis. In her leader, the editor deplored such vile behaviour, but cautioned against a rush to judgement. On the opinion page a younger member of the *Guardian* staff decreed that the victim was not only always right, but had a right to be believed.

Reading his copy of the paper that afternoon, alone in the Cabinet room, the prime minister found himself, on balance, siding with the latter. The more he read over his own work and admired the layout, the more convincing it became. He had to hand it to Jane. Such vicious, ruthless, heartless lying. Such an insult to real victims of masculine power. He wondered if he himself would ever have dared put his name to the article. Framed and confined within these pages, the story generated its own truth, rather in the way he imagined a nuclear reactor produced its own heat. Whether these things had happened or not, they might well have, they could so easily have, they were bound to have. They had! He was beginning to feel indignant on Jane's behalf. The foreign secretary was a wretch. Worse than that, he was late.

Five minutes later, when St John was shown in, Jim was still reading the pages, ostentatiously now, pen in hand. The two men did not exchange a greeting, nor did the prime minister stand. Instead he indicated the chair opposite him. At last, he folded the paper away, sighed and shook his head sadly. 'Well ... Benedict.'

The foreign secretary made no reply. He continued to stare steadily at Jim. It was disconcerting. To fill the silence the PM added, 'I'm not saying I believe a word of this.'

'But?' St John prompted. 'You're about to say but.'

'I am indeed. But, but and but. This isn't good for us. You know that. Until it's cleared up, I need you out the way.'

'Of course.'

There was silence again. Jim said kindly, 'I know how it used to be. Bit of malarkey behind the filing cabinet. Different times now. Me Too and all. There's your but. You have to go. That's final. I need your letter.'

St John reached across the table, pulled the newspaper towards him and opened it out. 'You were behind this.'

The PM shrugged. 'You leaked to the *Telegraph*.'

'Ours was all true. But yours!'

'Ours is true now, Benedict.' Jim glanced at his watch. 'Look, am I going to have to sack you?'

227

The foreign secretary took out a piece of paper folded in four and tossed it on the table.

Jim spread it out. Standard stuff. Great honour to have served ... baseless allegations ... distraction from the invaluable work of government.

'Good. So. Spend more time with your plotters.'

Benedict St John didn't even blink. 'We're going to fuck you up, Jim.'

In such exchanges it was important to have, if not the last word, then the last little touch. As the prime minister stood, he pressed a button under the table. It had been carefully arranged. A heavily bearded policeman came in, carrying an automatic rifle.

'Take him out the front way. And go slowly,' Jim said. 'Don't release his elbow until he's through the gates.'

The two men shook hands. 'They're waiting for you out there, Bennie. A photo-op. Would you like to borrow a comb?'

*

There was nothing in the near-infinite compendium of EU rules and trade protocols of the customs union that prevented a member state from reversing the circulation of its finances. That did not quite represent permission. Or did it? It was a defining principle of an open society that everything was lawful until there was a law against it. Beyond Europe's eastern borders, in Russia, China and all the totalitarian states of the world, everything was illegal unless the state sanctioned it. In the corridors of the EU, no one had ever thought of excluding the reverse flow of money from acceptable practice because no one had ever heard of the idea. Even if someone had, it would have been difficult to define the legal or philosophical principles by which it should be illegal. An appeal to basics would not have helped. Everyone knew that in every single law of physics, except one, there was no logical reason why the phenomena described could not run backwards as well as forwards. The famous exception was the second law of thermodynamics. In that beautiful construct, time was bound to run in one direction only. Then Reversalism was a special case of the second law and therefore in breach of it! Or was it? This question was hotly debated in the Strasbourg Parliament right up until the morning the members had to decamp to Brussels, as they frequently had to. By the time they had arrived and unpacked and enjoyed a decent lunch, everyone had lost the thread, even when a theoretical physicist came specially from the CERN laboratories to set everything straight in less than three hours with some interesting equations. Besides, the next day a further question arose. Would what the scientist said remain true if he'd said it in reverse?

The matter, like many others, was set aside. A fierce debate on Moldovan ice cream was pending. The issue was not as trivial as the Europhobe London press was pretending. The struggle to harmonise the ingredients of the high-quality Moldovan product with EU rules represented a microcosm of growing diplomatic tensions between the west and Russia over the future of the tiny, strategically placed country. It was a complex business but, in theory at least, it was solvable. Reversalism was beyond all that.

The average Brussels official had watched in wonder as the startling decision was made by referendum. Then, after all, one tended to relax and shrug as the whole process predictably stalled, mired in complexity. Surely, this nonsense was about to be shelved in the time-honoured fashion. But lately there was even greater wonder as kindly, dithering Prime Minister Sams appeared to undergo a personality change to emerge as a modern Pericles, artful and ferocious in driving Reversalism through, do or die, with or without Europe. Was it really going to happen? Couldn't the mother of parliaments bring the nation to its senses? Could it really be the case that a fellow from Brussels in need of recreation could spend a lavish weekend at the London Ritz, then walk away from the check-out desk with three thousand pounds in his hand? And perhaps be arrested the same day for being in possession of illegal funds? Or at the least, have his funds confiscated as he left the country? Or – what horror – be obliged to buy a job in the hotel kitchens washing dishes until the cash was spent? How could a nation do this to itself? It was tragic. It was laughable. Surely the Greeks had a word for it, choosing to act in one's own very worst interests? Yes, they did. It was *akrasia*. Perfect. The word began to circulate.

But the puzzled, weary or condescending smiles began to freeze when the tweets of the US president assumed a degree of consistency on the subject. In the name of free trade, American prosperity and greatness, and raising the poor, Reversalism was 'good'. Prime Minister Sams was great. And, although by the conventions of EU subsidiarity this was strictly an internal affair, it bothered some in Brussels that President Tupper was proposing an ex-general, the billionaire owner of a string of casinos, to be the new 'czar' of the British National Health Service. For these various reasons the prime minister was listened to with unusual courtesy when he delivered a lecture at NATO headquarters in early December.

Sams was there in place of his disgraced foreign secretary. There was nothing new of substance in his talk except for its urgency. The PM came straight to the point. As everybody knew, the UK would be reversing its finances and therefore its fortunes on the twenty-fifth of that month. 'Save the date!' he called out cheerily. There were obliging smiles. The prime minister ran through a list of demands, long familiar to the negotiators among the audience in the grand lecture hall. The first of the EU's new annual contributions to the UK of £11.5 billion would fall due on 1 January. Nato's first payment was not expected until June. The funds that would accompany all EU exports to the UK must assume an inflation rate of two per cent. And to repeat – and here Jim spread his hands as though to embrace them all – as a gesture of goodwill, funds accompanying UK exports to the EU would match that rate. There were further technicalities as well as reassurances about the United States' 'direction of travel'. In his closing remarks, Jim expressed the hope that before long 'the scales would drop from your eyes', a phrase that flummoxed the Bulgarian interpreter in her booth at the back of the hall. The scales would drop, the prime minister said, and everyone would 'follow us blindly into the future'.

Afterwards, a young French diplomat was overheard saying to a colleague as they made their way to the banquet, 'I don't understand why they stood to applaud. And so loudly, and for so long.'

'Because,' his older companion explained, 'they detested everything he said.'

It was not unreasonable for the British press to describe Jim's speech as a triumph.

There was a disconcerting moment the next day in Berlin. He was there for a private meeting with the chancellor. It was a busy day for her in the Reichstag and, with much apology, she met with him in a tiny sitting room near her office. Apart from two interpreters, two notetakers, three bodyguards, the German foreign minister, the British ambassador and the second secretary, they were alone. Where they sat, an ancient oak table separated the two leaders. Everyone else was obliged to stand. Over the chancellor's shoulder the PM had a view across the Spree towards a museum. Through its plate glass windows, he could see a display of the history of the Berlin Wall. Jim knew two words in German: Auf and Wiedersehen. Halfway through the meeting, he was setting out his stall. He wanted extra funds to accompany German exports of cars to the UK in return for extra funds to supplement British exports of Glaswegian

Riesling which, as he explained, was far superior to the Rhenish version.

It was at this point that the chancellor interrupted him. With her elbow on the table, she pressed a hand to her forehead and closed her tired eyes. '*Warum?*' she said, and followed this word with a brief tangle of others. And again, '*Warum ...*' and a longer tangle. Then the same again. And finally, still with her eyes closed, and her head sinking a little further towards the table, a simple, plaintive, '*Warum?*'

Tonelessly, the interpreter said, 'Why are you doing this? Why, to what end, are you tearing your nation apart? Why are you inflicting these demands on your best friends and pretending we're your enemies? Why?'

Jim's mind went blank. Yes, he was weary from so much travel. There was silence in the room. Across the river a line of schoolchildren was forming up behind a teacher to go into the museum. Standing right behind his chair, the British ambassador softly cleared her throat. It was stuffy. Someone should open a window. There drifted through the PM's mind a number of compelling answers, though he did not utter them. Because. Because that's what we're doing. Because that's what we believe in. Because that's what we said we'd do. Because that's what people said they wanted. Because I've come to the rescue. Because. That, ultimately, was the only answer: *because*.

Then reason began to seep back and with relief he recalled a word from his speech the evening before. 'Renewal,' he told her. 'And the electric plane.' After an anxious pause, it came in a rush. Thank God. 'Because, Madame Chancellor, we intend to become clean, green, prosperous, united, confident and ambitious!'

That afternoon he was on his way back to Tegel Airport, dozing in the back of the ambassador's limo, when his phone rang.

'Bad news, I'm afraid,' the chief whip said. 'I've threatened all I can. They know they'll be deselected. But a dozen or more have gone over to Benedict. Sacking has made him popular. And they don't believe Fish. Or they hate her anyway. The way things stand now we're more than twenty votes short ... Jim, are you there?

'I'm here,' he said at last.

'So.'

'I'm thinking.'

'Prorogue *pour mieux sauter?*'

'I'm thinking.'

He was gazing out of the bulletproof window. The driver, preceded and followed by the outriders, was taking a circuitous route down narrow green roads, past well-kept shacks with quarter-acre gardens, also nicely tended. Little second homes, he assumed. There was a particular greyness to Berlin. A smooth and pleasant grey. It was in the air, in the light sandy soil, in the speckled stonework. Even in the trees and grass and suburban herbaceous borders. It was the cool and spacious grey necessary to sustained thought. As he mused and the chief whip waited, Jim felt his heartbeat slowing and his thoughts arranging themselves into patterns as neat and self-contained as the little houses he was passing. It was as if he was in possession of an ancient brain that could solve any modern problem it confronted. Even without the deep resource of the pheromonal unconscious. Or of the trivial Internet. Without pen and paper. Without advisers.

He looked up. The procession of cars and motorbikes ushering the prime minister towards his waiting RAF jet had stopped to rejoin the main road. Just then, a question came to him. It seemed to drift up from the bottom of a well a hundred miles deep. How lightly and beautifully it rose to present itself. How easy it was to pose the question: who was it he loved most in all the world? Instantly, he knew the answer, and he knew exactly what he was going to do.

*

No one was surprised when Archie Tupper asked a business friend to organise an impromptu conference of Republican lawmakers and the various institutes and think tanks to which they were attached. These meetings were common, rather devout, well funded, patriotic and convivial. The general drift was pro-life, pro-second amendment, with a strong emphasis on free trade. Mining, construction, oil, defence, tobacco and pharmaceuticals were well represented. Jim now recalled that he himself had been a couple of times, before he became leader of the party. He had only fond memories of affable, portly types of a certain age, with their scented, closely shaven pink faces, gentlemen comfortable in their tuxes. (Few women attended and no people of colour.) One kindly fellow had pressed on him a generous invitation to a million-acre ranch in Idaho. Five minutes later, another promised him a welcome in an antebellum spread in Louisiana. Generous and friendly, they tended to be hostile to any mention of climate change and to international organisations like the UN, NATO and the EU. Jim had felt at home. It was inevitable that they would take a close interest in and help fund Britain's Reversalist project, though many thought it was better suited to a small country and not for the USA. But perhaps Tupper was about to convince them otherwise. British MPs of the right persuasion had often been invited in the past couple of years. But this hastily arranged conference was going to make reverse-flow finance its theme. The president would give a brief keynote speech. Among the international guests invited were forty pro-government Conservative MPs. The venue was a hotel in Washington that happened to belong to Archie Tupper, which was expected to give proceedings there a certain intimacy.

For the British contingent, the timing was inconvenient. The parliamentary timetable was full. The only conversation was Reversalism. There was much anxiety about the rebellion led by the treacherous ex-foreign secretary. The date set for the vote was 19 December. Constituency business always intensified around this time, and there were the usual Christmas engagements, as well as family gatherings. But this was a luxurious trip, first-class travel, suites measuring six thousand square feet, astonishing five-figure per diem expenses, a handshake with the president and overall excitement that American interest in the British Project was growing. On top of that, the prime minister had written to them all personally, urging them to attend. He wasn't going himself. Instead he was sending in his place Trevor Gott, the chancellor of the Duchy of Lancaster, a dull fellow, occasionally impulsive, often described as being 'two-dimensional'. There was nothing for it – the MPs made their apologies to colleagues, constituency officials and families and set about making their 'pairing' arrangements. This was a parliamentary convention by which a member who had to be absent from the house for a vote could pair off with an MP of the opposing benches. Neither would attend, and so the vote could not be affected. It was particularly useful for MPs on the government side who were often away on official business. Useful too for MPs who were ill or demented or attending funerals.

The conference was a stunning success, as they almost always are. At the start, President Tupper said that the British prime minister was great, and Reversalism was good. Among the congressmen and senators, oligarchs and think-tank intellectuals, there was a joyous sense that the world was configuring itself to their dreams. History was on their side. The banquet on the evening of 18 December was as magnificent as the several banquets that preceded it. After the speeches, a full orchestra backed a Frank Sinatra imitator in a soaring rendition of 'My Way'. Then a Gloria Gaynor lookalike brought seven hundred tearful diners to their feet with 'I Will Survive'.

Just as everybody was sitting down, the phones of forty guests vibrated in unison. They were urgently commanded by the chief whip to return to London. Their ground transport was already outside the hotel. Their flight was leaving in two hours. They had ten minutes to pack. They were needed in the Commons by eleven the next morning for the crucial Reversalism vote. The pairing arrangement had broken down.

The British left the banqueting room with no time for farewells to their new friends. How they cursed their Labour colleagues all the way to Ronald Reagan Airport. What an outrage, to be dragged from paradise by the perfidy of those they had foolishly trusted. Since most of the MPs were too angry to sleep, they punished the drinks trolley and cursed all the way to Heathrow. Due to heavy traffic around Chiswick, they arrived in the Commons just a few minutes before the Division Bell rang. Only as the Washington Revellers, as they came to be known, filed through the lobby did they notice the absence of their pairing partners. The Bill was passed with a majority of twenty-seven votes. The rest, as people kept saying all through the morning, was 'history'. The next day, the Reversalism Bill received Royal Assent and passed into law.

It was, of course, a constitutional scandal, a disgrace. Howls of rage from the Clockwiser press. The forty paired Labour MPs signed a letter to the *Observer* angrily denouncing the Sams government's 'filthy, shameless manoeuvrings'. There were calls for a judicial review.

'We'll ride it out. It will be fine. Just you see,' Jim told Jane Fish on the phone. Afterwards, he arranged for a case of champagne to be sent round to the chief whip's office.

That evening he gave a long interview to BBC television. He said in grave, reasonable tones, 'Apologise? Let me explain the fundamentals. In this country we do not have a written constitution. What we have instead are traditions and conventions. And I have always honoured them, even when to do so has been against my best interests. Now, I should point out to you that there is a long and honourable tradition in the house of breaking the pairing arrangement. Not so long ago, but before my time as prime minister, a Liberal Democrat MP was giving birth to her baby while her pairing partner, on the instruction of the whips, was voting in the Commons on a closely contested matter. As is well known, back in 1976 the highly respected Michael Heseltine picked up and swung the mace in the Chamber in celebration, one might say, of a broken pair. Twenty years later three of our MPs were paired not only with three absent Labour MPs but also with three Lib Dems. Labour has broken the pairing arrangement on countless occasions. They're only too happy to tell you about it late at night in the Strangers' Bar. All these examples bind into place a convention of cheating that has passed into common practice. It is constitutionally correct. It shows the world that parliament is, above all, a fine and fallible place, warm and vibrant with the human touch. I should also add that pairing is far less common in important votes. It was quite right to bring those MPs back from Washington to the Commons when a matter of vital national importance was at stake. Of course, the opposition is crying foul. That's their job. Some of them are miffed that Horace Crabbe voted with us. So, in answer to your question, no, emphatically no, neither I nor any members of my government have anything to apologise for.'

It wasn't a white Christmas, but it was not far off. There was a light fall on the first of January, just before the R-Day bank holiday. Two inches of snow deterred no one. Millions rushed to the stores to lay in money to pay for their jobs when they returned to work after the break. There were a few expected teething problems. Fans turned up for a Justin Bieber concert expecting to be paid. The event was cancelled. People stood by cash machines wondering whether they were supposed to poke cash into the slot formerly intended for debit cards.

But these were the largest January sales on record. Shops were stripped clean of goods – a great boost to the economy some thought. The news that St Kitts and Nevis was withdrawing from the trade deal was barely noticed.

The prime minister, still in the Christmas spirit and looking rakish in a pink paper crown, sprawling shoeless in an armchair, neat whisky in hand, watched, along with a few of his staff, helicopter shots of mile-long queues along Oxford Street. He would have liked to say it out loud, but he let the words murmur in his thoughts: it was over; his job was done. Soon he would assemble his colleagues and inform them that it was time to begin the long march to the palace and be welcomed as heroes by their tribe.

*

In the afternoon, before the last Cabinet meeting, the PM sent all the staff home and arranged for the policeman on the front door to keep it ajar. All Cabinet members were to leave their borrowed bodies tidily at their ministry desks, ready for the return of their rightful owners. Jim left his own body on the bed upstairs. Thus, for the meeting itself, he imposed a strict dress code: exoskeletons. He had thought it would be fitting to convene on the Cabinet room table, but once they had assembled in the room, it looked an awfully long way up and rather tricky, since the table legs were highly polished. So they gathered in a corner of the room behind a wastepaper bin and stood in a proud circle. The PM was about to launch on his opening remarks but was cut off by a rendition of 'Happy Birthday', sung in lusty unharmonious chirrups. Afterwards they looked nervously towards the door. The duty policeman had not heard them.

The Cabinet meeting was conducted in pheromone, which runs at ten times the speed of standard English. Before Jim could speak, Jane Fish proposed a vote of thanks. She praised the PM's 'single-mindedness coupled, unusually, with rambunctious charm and humour.' Britain now stood alone. The people had spoken. The genius of our party leader had got them over the line. Their destiny was in their hands. Reversalism was delivered! No more dithering and delay! Britain stood alone!

As she called out the beloved slogans she was overcome with emotion and could not go on, but it did not matter. Rising applause, an earnest susurration of carapaces and vestigial wings greeted her words. Then each Cabinet minister added a few words, ending with the new foreign secretary, Humphrey Batton, recently promoted from the Ministry of Defence. He led everybody in a round of 'For He's a Jolly Good Fellow'.

To give his speech, the PM stepped into the centre of the circle. As he spoke, his antennae quivered with passion and he rotated slowly on the spot to catch everyone's attention.

'My dear colleagues, thank you for these kind thoughts. They touch me deeply. In these closing moments of our mission, our duty is to the truth. There is one that we have never concealed from our brilliant citizens. For the mighty engines of our industry, finance and trade to go into reverse, they must first slow and stop. There will be hardship. It might be punishing in the extreme. I don't doubt that enduring it will harden the people of this great country. But that is no longer our concern. Now that we have cast off our temporary, uncongenial forms, there are deeper truths that we may permit ourselves to celebrate.

'Our kind is at least three hundred million years old. Merely forty years ago, in this city, we were a marginalised group, despised, objects of scorn or derision. At best, we were ignored. At worst, loathed. But we kept to our principles, and very slowly at first, but with gathering momentum, our ideas have taken hold. Our core belief remained steadfast: we always acted in our own best interests. As our Latin name, *blattodea*, suggests, we are creatures that shun the light. We understand and love the dark. In recent times, these past two hundred thousand years, we have lived alongside humans and have learned their particular taste for that darkness, to which they are not as fully committed as we are. But whenever it is predominant in them, so we have flourished. Where they have embraced poverty, filth, squalor, we have grown in strength. And by tortuous means, and much experiment and failure, we have come to know the preconditions for such human ruin. War and global warming certainly and, in peacetime, immoveable hierarchies, concentrations of wealth, deep superstition, rumour, division, distrust of science, of intellect, of strangers and of social cooperation. You know the list. In the past we have lived through great adversity, including the construction of sewers, the repulsive taste for clean water, the elaboration of the germ theory of disease, peaceful accord between nations. We have indeed been diminished by these and many other depredations. But we have fought back. And now, I hope and believe that we have set in train the conditions of a renaissance. When that peculiar madness, Reversalism, makes the general human population poorer, which it must, we are bound to thrive. If decent, good-hearted, ordinary people have been duped and must suffer, they will be much consoled to know that other decent, good-hearted, ordinary types like ourselves will enjoy greater happiness even as our numbers grow. The net sum of universal wellbeing will not be reduced. Justice remains a constant.

'You have worked hard on our mission these past months. I congratulate and thank you. As you have discovered, it is not easy to be *Homo sapiens sapiens*. Their desires are so often in contention with their intelligence. Unlike us who are whole. You have each put a human shoulder to the wheel of populism. You have seen the fruits of your labour, for that wheel is beginning to turn. Now, my friends, it is time to make our journey south. To our beloved home! Single file please. Remember to turn left as you go out the door.'

He did not mention it, but he knew that every minister in his Cabinet understood the perils that lay ahead. It was just after 4 p.m. on a cloudy afternoon when they slipped through the open door and past the duty policeman. They welcomed the winter gloom. Because of it, they did not see the little creature scurrying towards Number Ten to resume its life. Within half an hour Jim's group was passing under the gates of Downing Street into Whitehall. They crossed the pavement and climbed down into the gutter. The mountain of horse dung had long gone. The moving forest of rush-hour feet thundered above them. It took ninety minutes to reach Parliament Square and it was here that tragedy struck. They were waiting for the lights to change and were preparing to make their dash across the road. But Trevor Gott, the chancellor of the Duchy of Lancaster, got ahead of himself, as he sometimes did, and ran out too soon and disappeared under the wheel of a rubbish truck. When the traffic stopped the entire Cabinet ran out into the road to help him. He lay on his back, truly two-dimensional. From under his shell, there was extruded a thick, off-white creamy substance, a much-loved delicacy. There would be a heroes' banquet that night and what fun it would be, with so many extraordinary stories to tell. Before the lights changed again, his colleagues had just enough time to pick him up and place the extrusion reverently on his underbelly. Then, with six ministers each taking a leg, they bore him away to the Palace of Westminster.

Ian McEwan
The Cockroach
Copyright © Ian McEwan 2019
This edition arranged with ROGERS，COLERIDGE & WHITE LTD(RCW)
through Big Apple Agency，Inc.，Labuan，Malaysia.
Simplified Chinese edition copyright：
2021 Shanghai Translation Publishing House（STPH）
ALL RIGHTS RESERVED.

图字：09‐2020‐831号

图书在版编目(CIP)数据

蟑螂：汉、英／(英)伊恩·麦克尤恩
(Ian McEwan)著；宋金译. — 上海：上海译文出版社，
2021.5
(麦克尤恩双语作品)
书名原文：The Cockroach
ISBN 978‐7‐5327‐8634‐3

Ⅰ.①蟑… Ⅱ.①伊… ②宋… Ⅲ.①中篇小说—英国—现代—汉、英 Ⅳ.①I561.45

中国版本图书馆CIP数据核字(2021)第050650号

蟑螂
[英]伊恩·麦克尤恩 著 宋 金 译
责任编辑／宋 玲 装帧设计／张志全工作室

上海译文出版社有限公司出版、发行
网址：www.yiwen.com.cn
200001 上海福建中路193号
上海义艺人一印刷有限公司印刷

开本787×1092 1/32 印张8 插页6 字数43,000
2021年6月第1版 2021年6月第1次印刷
印数：0,001—6,000册

ISBN 978‐7‐5327‐8634‐3/I·5332
定价：69.00元

本书中文简体字专有出版权归本社独家所有,非经本社同意不得转载、摘编或复制
本书如有质量问题,请与承印厂质量科联系。T：021‐64511411